Dimensions of Design – 100 Classical Seats

Vitra Design Museum

Dimensions of Design - 100 Classical Seats

This publication is an accompaniment to the miniatures exhibition "Dimensions of Design - 100 Classical Seats", an exhibition presented by the **Vitra Design Museum**, Weil am Rhein, in co-operation with the GOETHE INSTITUT, Munich.

Exhibition

Concept: Alexander von Vegesack, Matthias Kries

Curator: Matthias Kries

Production of miniatures: Thomas Schweikert, Miroslaw Melerski

Design: Dieter Thiel

Responsible on behalf of the Goethe Institute: Dr. Wolfger Pöhlmann

Tour organization in Asia, Africa: Susanne Niemann, Goethe Institute

Tour organization in Europe, USA, Latin America: Vitra Design Museum

Catalogue

Publisher: Alexander von Vegesack

Text contributions: Matthias Kries, Mathias Schwartz-Clauss, Dr. Peter Dunas,

Dr. Petra Rohde, Federica Zanco

Design: Thorsten Romanus

Drawings: Bernard Monestier, Beatrice Brengues

Translations: Jeremy Gaines, Ann Thursfield-Stinglwagner

Printing: Grafisches Zentrum Drucktechnik, Ditzingen (D)

Dimensions of Design –
100 Classical Seats

Notes on the technical details of the objects:

The manufacturers' details name the first producer of the object.
The production data refers to this production.
Other manufacturers are, for the main part, mentioned in the text.
In most cases, the miniature focuses on objects from the first production.

Dimensions of Design -
A miniature exhibition of the Vitra Design Museum

From time immemorial man has altered the scale of an object if he wants to influence the observer's perception. There are varied motives for this.

In socialist countries, for example, overdimensional buildings were erected in order to suggest awe and subordination to man by means of monumental architecture. Pop-Art artist Claes Oldenbourg works with giant stylized objects and uses these to analyze the connection between scale and meaning in his motifs. The scaling down of an object, on the other hand, can have a purely practical purpose, for instance in the case of designers and engineers who, with the example of small draft models, test constructions and develop new forms. Miniatures can, however, also trigger off complex phenomena in the perception of the observer. For example, small objects and toys remove a child's fear of the size of the adult world and make the environment "graspable". The aspect of the controllable world of objects, spread out before the observer, also plays an important role in other forms of miniaturising, fulfilling a deeply-rooted need for power and security. Small fetishes or statuettes illustrate that diminuitives can also have a cultic and excessive meaning for man. In this case miniaturising is equated with a process in which powers become concentrated and the object receives magical significance.

The attractiveness of the chair miniatures which the Vitra Design Museum has been producing since 1992 is founded on their small-scale size. As reproductions of the most famous seats to the scale of 1:6, true to the original and precisely corresponding to the model with regard to workmanship, detail and material, they have become much sought-after collectors' articles. Some of these chairs, such as Le Corbusier's chaise longue or the red-blue chair by Gerrit Rietveld, are as well-known nowadays as the most famous works of art. And just as high-quality reprints are made of a painting, the Vitra Design Museum miniaturises chairs in three dimensional form - as a witness to an age and as an ideal object of study.

The miniature conveys more than pure information value which a media image can provide. It triggers off a process of discovery. On the one hand it is irritating since it has no utility value as a seat and in this respect is therefore not able to uphold the promise of the original. This arouses the question as to what actually goes to make a good chair. On the other hand the eyes are at once directed, as a result of the technically perfect precision work, to constructive connections, screws, supports or joins. Besides, a chair is visually more easily ascertainable as a miniature and its proportions stand out more clearly. A different, in a sense a closer relationship therefore emerges than in the case of utility furniture which is in daily use. The observer examines the miniature with technical interest but also with the curiosity which small things have triggered off in us since our childhood. His eyes are challenged and sharpened but not deceived.

In the exhibition on display here 100 classical seats convey the meaning of design and the role it plays in the industrial production process. Moreover the exhibits provide information on the social, cultural and economic developments of their age since the chair plays a central role in man's everyday life and also acts as a reflection of it. Almost all great designers or architects have tried thier hand in this field. They have felt challenged not only by the high static demands of the chair but also by its close relationship to the human anatomy. As the chair is used for the most varied purposes in the private field and also in public buildings or at the workplace, it illustrates in an ideal fashion the complex demands placed on an industrial product.

In this respect Model No. 14 by Thonet from the year 1860 still retains a model role even today. It was one of the first successful attempts to think through a product economically, constructively and aesthetically from draft to dispatch. Industrial aesthetics received a new impulse in the Twenties with the discovery of the steel tube for furniture building. In 1925 Marcel Breuer built the first piece of tubular steel furniture with his chair B3, and shortly afterwards Ludwig Mies van der Rohe drafted the first cantilevered chair from this material. The furniture drafts from the Fifties and Sixties also provide a focus of the exhibition. During this epoch furniture design experienced a spread of synthetic substances, prepared for by the experiments of Charles and Ray Eames. The structural freedom given to the designer by synthetic materials signified a highlight but, at the same time, a turning point of the modern movement. The colourful experiments of the Sixties were followed by a reflection upon historical styles, ecological processes and individual forms of expression. The juxtaposition of these varied approaches also determines contemporary design.

A selection of key objects co-determining the causes and backgrounds of the developments mentioned briefly here were shown in 1995 in the exhibition "100 Masterpieces from the Vitra Design Museum Collection". Since such an exhibition, which includes delicate originals, is very expensive and elaborate, a corresponding miniature exhibition has been developed. Thanks to the miniaturisied exhibits it has been possible to produce four sets of this exhibition which will run parallel to each other and be shown world-wide as of June 1997. We are especially pleased that the non-European tour will take place in co-operation with the Goethe Institute. The widespread-linking infrastructure of the individual Goethe Institutes and their cultural reputation will contribute toward informing a large audience about the history of furniture design by means of this exhibition. Perhaps the concentrated, clear world of miniatures will help the visitor to better orientate himself in the diversity of styles of contemporary design.

Alexander von Vegesack
Vitra Design Museum
Director

Matthias Kries
Vitra Design Museum
Curator

Can a Seat be Classical?

Every selection of objects for an exhibition is as such an expression of a special form of esteem. The title of our exhibition in connection with the magical number 100 and the concept of the classical element serves to heighten even further this form of high regard. The label "classical" is, after all, connected in our minds with only historically-backed, indeed with exemplary achievements of our culture outliving all ages.

Of all consumer items in the human living space, the seat is something very special. It is the one object which, with respect to its design, is the most closely related to the human body; and it is not by chance that this form, from the beginnings of human development sometimes even until today is linked to the status of its owners. In archaic cultures and epochs the common people had to sit on the floor. The use of chairs, stools etc. was the exclusive privilege of dignitaries and rulers and all seats were designed in a correspondingly elaborate fashion. Up to our age this element has remained evident above all in public areas in which, from the throne to the boss's chair, seats still symbolize hierarchies.
It should therefore be no surprise that up to the present day creating a seat still represents a particular challenge to artists, architects and designers, reaching far beyond the otherwise determining functional element of consumer goods. No other piece of furniture can show such a comparable diversity of form as the chair, stool and armchair, and correspondingly diverse are also the specialized terms which either refer to function e.g. dining-room chair, bar stool and club chair, to form or composition e.g. board-chair, rung-chair, box-seat, bentwood chair, stack or console chair or cantilevered chair or to the materials e.g. basketwork, wickerwork, fabric, leather, wood, metal and plastic. The 100 examples of the most varying kinds of seats presented in the exhibition as scaled-down miniature sculptures, true to the original, just like objects of art on pedestals under glass covers at eye-level, provide an impressive image of the scope of variation and structural imagination of their creators.

Although Germany has sent out important impulses for design development during our century, above all due to the Bauhaus, and although a museum located in Germany has produced this exhibition which, with the support of the Goethe Institute will be travelling round the world, German designers are in a minority. The exhibition shows in an almost exemplary fashion how, in the field of design and modern goods production, all national boundaries and categories per se have dissolved. For many years now it has been completely normal for technical production, design, material and consumers to stem from completely different countries. In this respect this exhibition is a stroke of luck for the Goethe Institute which is interested in an international cultural dialogue and, in co-operation with the Vitra Design Museum, would like to take the occasion of this exhibition for theme-related accompanying events in the form of seminars, discussions and workshops.

The Vitra Design Museum, situated at the crossroads of three countries, France, Switzerland and Germany, is recognised world-wide not only as being a result of an exemplary enterprise culture but it is also a perfect example of how, through the combined action of the best designers, artists and architects of our time, it is possible to produce exhibitions on constantly new realms of experience.

The most important function of this exhibition remains, however, the conveying and sharpening of criteria by the sensory experience of the selected exhibits for a task every one of us is set - the co-determining of the aesthetic quality and form of our environment.

Wolfger Pöhlmann
Goethe Institute
Head of Exhibitions Section

Shaker
Thonet
Van de Velde
Loos

1

Until 1900

From Cottage Craft to Industrial Production

In the first half of the 19th century the **industrial revolution** took place, changing things in all walks of human life to an hitherto inconceivable extent. The growing self-confidence of the bourgeoisie vis-à-vis the ruling aristocracy and a wave of new inventions had, ever since the 17th century, already caused a gradual reorganization of society and the world of work. When **James Watt** developed the first functioning **steam-engine** in 1783 and thus tapped a source of energy that did not depend on ambient conditions to drive machines, it was a decisive step forward in industrialization. This process spread from England in the early 19th century and by 1850 had also caught on in the other wealthy countries of Europe.

The potential industrial production offered for furniture builders was recognized at an early date by **Michael Thonet** (2, 4) , a cabinetmaker. As of around 1836, he consistently endeavored to streamline production processes for his furniture; in 1856, he founded the first factory in which furniture was industrially manufactured. Thonet managed to do this not least because he advanced the **bentwood technology** of his day, enabling rods of solid wood to be bent to form complex, three-dimensional forms, instead of carving them in the traditional, labor-intensive manner. When he died, Thonet left behind a company, which, thanks to the economic organization of all areas in it, became a model many companies tried to follow. Moreover, the emerging furniture industry was also characterized by the transition from work on commission to the production of a certain **line of goods** and the fact that a large part of the work was now handled by unskilled **factory workers** rather than skilled craftsmen.

The rapid development of the metal-working industry, the main locomotive of progress ever since the early days of the industrial revolution, also impacted on furniture building. Because of its resilience to bad weather, **furniture made of cast or bent iron** was used especially for gardens (5).

The academic art schools of the second half of the 19th century were dominated by a stylistic **eclecticism**. Almost by way of reaction to the explosive developments in industry and technology, many painters, sculptors and architects invoked a return to historical styles, which they quoted and combined at random. This **historicist** movement also spawned an important branch of the furniture industry, which supplied a rapidly growing market with richly decorated furniture, mainly assembled from pre-turned components.

The **Arts and Crafts movement**, by contrast, championed by **William Morris**, sought to animate the arts and crafts as an alternative to the gradual influx of anonymous industrial products. The members had their designs transformed into high-grade products using traditional crafts methods.

This gap between utilization and rejection of modern design means can also be discerned in the case of **Art Nouveau**. Artists like **Henry van de Velde** (7) drew the inspiration for their works in architecture, graphic arts, or the crafts from organic curved forms as well as Japanese and African motives, on the one hand, and the modern steel-girder constructions of factories or the Eiffel Tower, on the other.

One model espoused by those movements at the **fin de siècle** which took a critical stance toward progress, was the *"gesamtkunstwerk"*. Architecture, painting, sculpture and the applied arts all combined here to form a homogeneous interior and overcome the growing alienation of people from an increasingly anonymous environment.

In the United States, the transformation of the new technological possibilities came up against fewer traditions than in Europe. **Louis Sullivan**, who in the last quarter of the 19th century built the first **skyscrapers** in Chicago, caught the spirit of the day in his statement that **"form follows function"** - a maxim of 20th century design.

1

Name:	**Windsor Chair**
Designer:	**anonymous**
Draft:	**early 18th century**
Production:	**first half of the 19th century**
Manufacturer:	**anonymous, perhaps in Lincolnshire, England**
Measurements:	**H 92; W 54.5; D 58 cms**
Materials:	**solid bent yew, solid bent elm**

In the 17th century, French garden culture made its way to England, where gardens became a showcase for aristocratic and bourgeois life. While the magnificent gardens of the nobility often featured seats hewn from stone, or chairs on wheels, most middle-class garden owners required lightweight, inexpensive garden furniture.

The Windsor Chair was created to meet this need. It was probably developed in the early 18th century based on the above-mentioned garden chairs on wheels. The wheels of these chairs may have been the model on which the then-novel spoke construction in the back-rest of the Windsor Chair was based; the latter featured vertical struts that were stabilized by the arch that contained them and by the armrests. Prior to this, back-rests were usually carved from solid boards, which was very labor-intensive.

The arch in the back-rest of the Windsor Chair was created either by boiling solid wood in water and bending it into the desired shape, or by joining together a number of pieces of wood to create the desired form. The legs and cross struts were lathe-turned, and the seat was carved from solid wood in a shape that fitted the human body. Finally, the lathe-turned and carved elements were joined together, and the bent components in the construction were braced if they failed to retain their shape on their own.

Thanks to this simple procedure, it was possible to make chairs using elements that had been manufactured beforehand, heralding the division of labour in furniture production. The traditional craftsman's method required that the entire chair be manufactured in the course of a single working cycle by one person, whereas now individual steps could be delegated and performed separately.

At times, even farmers produced the individual parts for the chairs ahead of time and thus ensured that they would have an additional source of income during the winter months. By contrast, final assembly often took place in larger factories using cheap, unskilled labour in order to lower production costs.

As a result of this efficient procedure, the chairs were being produced in great numbers by the early 1800s. This was the basis for industrial furniture production as developed by German manufacturer Michael Thonet in the second half of the 19th century. The lively trade between England and the American colonies soon brought the chair to America, where it was first referred to as the "Windsor Chair". This epithet was used to describe all wooden chairs with a carved seat into which the back-rest construction and the lathe-turned legs were inserted. For a long time, the chair was only to be found in English-speaking countries, where it was used not only for gardens, but also in pantries and kitchens; other variations also appeared, for example rocking chairs or children's chairs. In the latter half of the 19th century, bentwood furniture producers on the Continent, such as Gebr. Thonet and J. & J. Kohn, began producing and selling Windsor Chairs. Toward the end of the 19th century, a number of fashionable and odd versions of the Windsor chair appeared, for example sporting Victorian, neo-Gothic or classical Greek decor. MK

2

Name:	**Bopparder Stuhl**
Designer:	**Michael Thonet**
Draft:	**approx. 1836**
Manufacturer:	**Michael Thonet, Boppard**
Production:	**approx. 1836-42**
Measurements:	**H 85.5; W 42.5; D 50 cms**
Materials:	**laminated veneerstrips, joined, veneered wood, cane**

Michael Thonet opened his first carpentry and joinery workshop in 1819, at the age of 23. The furniture initially produced there was not stylistically innovative, but instead followed the curved, antiquated forms preferred by the up-and-coming middle classes in the late Biedermeier period.
The light, stable frame used for these chairs and armchairs soon became popular far beyond the limits of the town of Boppard. It consists of a seat frame, two side supports and four cross struts. The seat frame was traditionally carved from solid wood, and either upholstered or covered with wicker, which enhanced the stability of the seat and meant that a more slender frame could be used.
In achieving the desired form for the side supports, however, Thonet employed a technique that was hitherto virtually unknown in furniture design. Bundles of veneer strips were boiled in an adhesive solution to give them optimal pliability, and then placed in heated wooden

molds, where they remained until finally dry, whereby they retained the molded shape.
The molds which Thonet initially used to bend the veneer strips permitted the side supports to be formed only on a two-dimensional plane. However, they were already wide enough to allow several identical pieces to be cut from one molded piece per working cycle. In addition, the production of the chairs was already so organized that the frames and back-rest could be interchanged, in other words formal variety was possible.
The layer of veneer then applied made the chair look as if it were made of solid wood, for all traces of the clever laminating process had been concealed.
Over the subsequent decades, Michael Thonet continued refining the technique used in producing the Boppard Chair. In around 1860, he succeeded in making chairs out of solid wood bent in three dimensions, marking the decisive step toward industrial furniture production. MK

3

Name: (Shaker Chair)
Designer: anonymous
Draft: around 1840
Production: as of approx. 1840
Manufacturer: different craftsmen in the Shaker communities
Measurements: H 110.5; W 47; D 37; seating height 44.5 cms
Materials: wood, fabric covers

The "Shakers" were a religious movement, founded by the Englishwoman Ann Lee. Lee emigrated with some followers from Manchester (England) to the United States in 1774 and settled in the state of New York. The name derives from a ritual and "shaking" dance which the group performed. The religious sect lived in large families, had no notion of private property, wore strict, plain clothes and almost exclusively provided for itself. Despite furious hostilities toward them, the number of followers grew continually, so that by 1840 approx. 6,000 Shakers lived in 18 different settlements. They quickly gained recognition for their exemplary conduct as American citizens and their high standards of craftsmanship. The products manufactured by them stemmed from their belief that only through their own work could they create a harmonious and contemplative environment, a "paradise on earth".
While the manufacture of furniture was originally only intended to cover their own needs, it soon formed the

chief source of income for many of the Shaker communities. The plain, but high-quality workmanship of the furniture vividly illustrated the Shakers' rejection of superficial decoration and comfort. For their common rooms, in which they took their meals, celebrated services, carried out handiwork or rested, the Shakers needed versatile and easily transportable chairs. If they were not used, they were hung from the walls to save space. The one shown here is an all-purpose chair without armrests, manufactured with minor changes by the communities in Pleasant Hill (Kentucky), New Lebanon (New York), and Sabbathday Lake (Mains). In addition to this basic model, variants existed such as a rocking chair, a child's chair, an armchair and a stool.
As early as the 19th century, European furniture companies such as Gebr. Thonet also produced furniture in the Shaker style. The trend in recent years in favour of a lifestyle oriented to nature has led to numerous furniture manufacturers including Shaker style models in their collections. MK

4

Name:	**Chair No. 14**
Designer:	**Michael Thonet and Sons**
Draft:	**1859/60**
Production:	**1865 to the present**
Manufacturer:	**Gebrüder Thonet, Vienna**
Measurements:	**H 92.5; W 42; D 50; seat height 46.5 cms**
Materials:	**bent beechwood, cane**

Worldwide, "No. 14" is one of the most successful products in the history of industrial mass production. It also established the international reputation of the Thonet Company. By 1930 over 50 million units of the chair had already been sold. In 1930 the price was DM 8.50 and this was the most reasonably priced model within the Thonet line. Even today it is being produced in modified form. Starting in 1830, Michael Thonet began to experiment with shaping laminated wood. He boiled wood strips in glue and bent them into prepared iron molds. He is recognized as the founder of industrial bentwood processing and in 1836 introduced the first chair made of laminated wood. Efficient methods of manufacturing, a reduction in the individual parts of a chair, and finally the development of its own distribution network via sales offices in all major cities around the globe enabled Thonet to develop into an international company. Laminated and molded wooden furniture sold in subtropical countries with high humidity led to a flood of complaints since the glue tended to dissolve. Because of this pressure, Michael Thonet developed a procedure of bending solid wood with steam, replacing the glued peg jointing with screws. Model "No. 14" was the first product utilizing this new bentwood technique and, after about 1865, the entire fabrication was switched over. Thanks to the screwed connections, it was now possible to ship the chairs in their individual parts for final assembly at their destination. Thirty-six dismantled "No. 14" chairs could be packed into a crate with a volume of only one cubic meter. Since the connections could be retightened as necessary, the lifespan of the chair was also enhanced as an added benefit. PD

5 

Name:	**(Bent Iron Chair)**
Designer:	**anonymous**
Draft:	**approx. 1865**
Production:	**approx. 1870-75**
Manufacturers:	**possibly Société des Hauts-Fourneaux et Fonderies du Val d'Osne, Paris, or Eisenmöbel-Fabrik Schorndorf, Württemberg**
Measurements:	**H 78.5; W 50.5; D 49 cms, seat height 40 cms**
Materials:	**round steel bars, sheet iron**

Iron has been used in furniture construction ever since the invention of forges. By the end of the 18th century, cast iron furniture was being produced in large quantities thanks to more advanced iron smelting technology, and thus began to find increasing use in gardens and parks. During the mid-19th century, furniture made of slender, bent iron rods came into fashion in the trend-setting city of Paris. The decisive advantage of bent iron furniture was not only that it was much less expensive and lightweight than cast-iron models, it was also easy to mold three-dimensionally, and, like bentwood furniture, could be produced in a wide variety of styles and patterns at low cost. Within a short time, a large number of competing iron furniture factories had sprung up, which often manufactured products so similar that it is difficult to attribute an individual model to a particular

manufacturer solely on the basis of its features.
While the iron chairs with their vertical cross struts initially took after the Windsor chairs in terms of shape, during the second half of the 19th century they began to incorporate the curved forms that adorned the back-rests of the bentwood chairs. The model shown here draws on the style of the Thonet chair No. 4.
The seat frame, made of interwoven iron strips or perforated iron sheets, normally rested on four identical side supports that converged to form the legs. Doubling the legs in this manner made the construction so stable that additional cross struts were unnecessary. The seat itself was probably covered with a removable cushion so that the chair could be left outdoors.
There were obvious advantages to iron furniture - it was inexpensive and absolutely impervious to weather. Simple, hygienic furniture was produced for hospitals and offices, camp beds and stretchers were manufactured for military purposes, while models with ornamental back-rests were preferred for outdoor cafés and private gardens, or as auxiliary seating. The iron furniture was the most popular in the country of its purported origin, France. But metal was rejected as a material for fashionable interior designs - until 1925, that is, when Marcel Breuer came up with the idea for his B 3 club chair, a design which made tubular steel the epitome of avant-garde aesthetics. MK

6

Name:	**Rocking Chair No. 9 (No. 809)**
Designer:	**(Firm draft)**
Draft:	**approx. 1882/83**
Production:	**approx. 1883-1926**
Manufacturer:	**Jakob & Josef Kohn, Vienna**
Measurements:	**H 104 W 63.5 D 116 cms**
Materials:	**bent beech wood, cane**

In the second half of the 19th century bentwood firms began to manufacture rocking chairs which, as a symbol of leisure and relaxation, corresponded to the need of the successful bourgeoisie for an appropriate level of comfort.

The prototype for the first rocking chair made of bentwood - model No. 1, produced around 1859 by the firm of Thonet - was most likely the so-called Winfield chair, a rocking chair made of iron and popular in England. Michael Thonet could possibly have become acquainted with this model during the 1851 world exhibition in London. Just as was the case with this forerunner, the supports between the back-rest and rockers of the Thonet rocking chair are a clear reminder that they were developed from the back legs of a conventional armchair. In a constructive and optical sense the side support elements are closely connected with the continuous line formed by the back-rest, seat and frame.

Around 1882/83 the firm of Jakob & Josef Kohn put a model onto the market which differentiated distinctly from earlier rocking chairs. A double loop, which clearly stands out against the framework, unites the supporting functions on either side. As a result of the above-mentioned back-leg-like supports being replaced by the smaller bentwood loop at the back, the construction of the chair takes on an elegant and weightless appearance. Among all the many kinds of ornaments with which the sides of conventional curved wood rocking chairs were decorated and, at the same time, supported, this solution is particularly simple and coherent. Rocking chair No. 9 (as from around 1903 No. 809) was produced until around 1926 with slight variations, for example with a foot support. The motif of the double loop was also applied to other models and became a typical feature of rocking chairs manufactured by J. & J. Kohn.

The firm, founded in 1867, had initially mainly copied Thonet furniture. Innovatory drafts, such as the model shown here, helped the business to develop its own original style. As of 1900, J. & J. Kohn began to increasingly concentrate on the geometrisized drafts of the Viennese architects. MK

7

Name:	**Bloemenwerf (Chair for the Bloemenwerf House)**
Designer:	**Henry Van de Velde**
Draft:	**1895**
Production:	**1895**
Manufacturer:	**Société Van de Velde, Brussels**
Measurements:	**H 93; W 47.5; D 47.5 cms**
Materials:	**wood, fabric upholstery**

Henry van de Velde was a Belgian who originally worked exclusively as a painter, until in 1889 he came across the ideas of British designer William Morris and thereafter became a self-taught craftsman and architect. Morris had founded the Arts & Crafts movement around 1860 in an attempt to revive traditional arts and crafts on the basis of a socialist outlook. Van de Velde mixed the farm-house thrust of Arts & Crafts furniture with the organic lines of the nascent Art Nouveau movement and, in the years that followed, produced furniture, clothing, tableware, lamps, textiles and prints. He had a considerable influence on turn-of-the-century design, and continued to have an impact long after the Art Nouveau era was over.

In 1895, Van de Velde designed and built the Bloemenwerf house for his wife and himself in Uccle, a suburb of Brussels. The building did not feature the highly stylised architecture that typified the 19th century, but instead, with its numerous windows, had a rustic, family feel to it. As the work of a self-taught architect, it caused a considerable stir and contributed much to van de Velde's fame.

Van de Velde also designed the interior, which he filled with simple, practical furniture. Van de Velde's dining room chair combined these attributes with a lightweight, elegant appearance. Thanks to its logical construction, with just a few formal alterations the design could be used to create an armchair, a simple chair, or a children's high chair. While the gentle curves in the legs and back-rest only minimally reveal van de Velde's dynamic, ornamented Art Nouveau designs, the influence of the Arts & Crafts furniture is clearly apparent in the reduced rod construction and the rustic bast covering.

This design possibly parallels the skeleton construction of the Eiffel tower, built only a short time earlier, which Van de Velde always admired during his numerous visits to Paris. Such a structure confirmed his opinion that the advance of industrial technology and the use of industrial materials called for a new, reduced approach to ornamentation. In fact, the only decorative aspect of van de Velde's chair is its carefully conceived structure. However, like all his designs, it was produced exclusively by hand in van de Velde's own furniture workshop. MK

8

Name:	**No. 255 (Chair for Café Museum)**
Designer:	**Adolf Loos**
Draft:	**around 1898**
Production:	**around 1899-1906**
Manufacturer:	**Jacob & Josef Kohn, Vienna**
Measurements:	**H 88.4; W 44; D 52.5 cms**
Materials:	**bent beechwood, cane**

Until 1896, Adolf Loos worked with Louis Sullivan, an American architect who was a pioneer in high-rise construction. After returning to Vienna, Loos initially became a journalist and earned a reputation as a vehement critic of the academicist school of art, which at the end of the 19th century often led to bizarre admixtures of various styles.

Designing the interior of Café Museum in 1897 offered him his first opportunity to implement his ideas. The result was a simple, minimalist interior that contrasted starkly with the exaggerated ostentation of fin-de-siècle Vienna. The bar and billiard tables made of dark wood were not ornamented with lathe work, but instead featured only smooth brass fittings. The light green wallpaper was not patterned, and the dark green of the billiard table cover contrasted with the color of the chairs, which were stained in a red hue instead of the usual dark tones. This unadorned setting made such an unusual and provocative impression on the public than the Café was dubbed "Café Nihilism".

In designing chairs to match the interior, Loos started with a well-known and conventional model, Chair No. 14 by Gebr. Thonet. Additional formal elements, illustrated in sketches of the designs by J. & J. Kohn, lent the Café Museum chair its striking form. Various models produced by the Kohn company sport the curved Art Nouveau back-rest and the rounded elements connecting it to the seat frame. The connecting elements between the seat frame and legs, which served to stabilize the construction, were also developed by J. & J. Kohn. The broadening of the feet is a feature taken from chairs made in the early 18th century, called "pied de biche" ("deerfoot"). Loos appropriated all these well-known elements, but also added an important structural innovation: He employed wood with an elliptical cross section, whereby the thickness increased at the points subject to greater stress, thus enhancing the stability of the chair. In addition, the alternating thickness of the rods lends the design a vitality that evokes the organic forms of Art Nouveau furniture.
The interior of Café Museum had a profound influence on architects like Josef Hoffmann, Kolomann Moser or Gustav Siegel. Loos' chair design features a seat of laminated wood instead of canework, and although it was only sold for a limited time, it is considered to mark the advent of the Viennese "architect designs" which were used by members of the Secession as of 1900 to create a fundamentally new shape for bentwood furniture. However, this chair does not anticipate the aesthetics of the "architect designs", and instead constitutes the final pinnacle in a series of classic bentwood furniture. MK

Mackintosh
Lee
Hoffmann
Wagner
Wright
Hofman
Rietveld

2

1900 to 1920

The first designers

While, at the beginning of the 20th century, **social problems** in Europe were the issue underlying many disputes between employers and employees, the US economy continued to grow uninhibitedly. As early as the last quarter of the 19th century, it was here that **Thomas A. Edison** invented the **electric bulb**, the **record player** and the **cinematograph**, while **Alexander Graham Bell** invented the **telephone** - objects which were to have a decisive influence on the 20th century. These products were quite without historical precedent, and instead radically new creations in terms of form and function, fully the product of the potential and needs of the new industrial society.
In general, the growing recognition of the importance of mechanization led to artists and designers focusing on more rational designs following the stylistic experiments of the close of the 19th century. While industrially produced furniture had, until then, mainly involved anonymous designs by the manufacturers, designers now increasingly tackled the problems of rational production. Since the profession of the designer as such did not yet exist, it was above all renowned architects such as **Josef Hoffmann** (12, 13, 14), **Gustav Siegel, Otto Wagner** (15) , **Kolomann Moser** or **Adolf Loos** (8), who, predominantly in Vienna, created the first items of furniture designed specially for industrial mass production. This **separation of design and production**

into two fundamentally different steps in the overall process, each handled by a specific person, is today often regarded as the moment when **design** proper was first born.

Following William Morris' lead, in 1903 Josef Hoffmann and Kolomann Moser founded the **"Wiener Werkstätte"** with the goal of enhancing cooperation between the designing artists and the craftsmen. However, they retained the rationalistic formal idiom vouchsafed by industry. Their products are often shaped using mainly geometric forms, so that some commentators spoke of the **"dictatorship of the square"**.

Another reason for the gradual disappearance of the traditional ornamental approach was the **inspiration** those handling the design work drew from **non-European cultures**; the latter prompted artists and designers to prefer clarity and expressiveness to the formal canon of the academic schools.

As a result, we find **Far Eastern influences** at work in the designs of representatives of Art Nouveau, such as **Charles Rennie Mackintosh** (9), but also in the oeuvre of **Frank Lloyd Wright** (16, 19), an architect who played such an important role in the 20th century. In Prague, architects and designers take up **Cubism**, inspired by Africa and otherwise a movement confined mainly to the fine arts: the upshot is an interesting stylistic phenomenon. Between 1910 and 1925, **Czech Cubism** generates a wealth of innovative objects and buildings, apparently assembled from geometric and crystalline forms (17).

A discussion in the year 1914, typical for the state of

design at the beginning of the 20th century, captures the different positions in industrial design at the beginning of the century. **Henry van de Velde** (7), the head of the arts-and-crafts college in Weimar, claimed that industrial production should not squeeze out the individual design of objects, while **Hermann Muthesius**, who had founded the German Werkbund in Munich in 1907, advocated standardization.

9

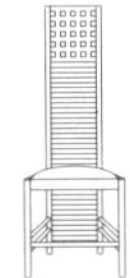

Name: Hill House (Chair for the Hill House)
Designer: Charles Rennie Mackintosh
Draft: 1903
Production: 1903
Manufacturer: possibly Francis Smith or Alexander Martin, Glasgow
Measurements: H 140; W 40.5; D 33.5 cms
Materials: black stained oak, velvet

Charles Rennie Mackintosh was one of the main proponents of Art Nouveau, and the most famous British designer at the beginning of the 20th century.
Although he had studied architecture, he also created a full range of furnishings for the interiors of his buildings, including furniture, cutlery, wallpaper and glassware.
His designs are a combination of floral, curved motifs and strictly geometric patterns, thus creating a brand of Art Nouveau that was uniquely his own. The ornamental aspects of Mackintosh's work were heavily influenced by his wife, painter Margaret McDonald, with whom he worked together closely. Together with Margaret's sister and brother-in-law, Frances and Herbert McNair, they founded an artists' group, "The Four", in 1890. The works of this group became known as the "Glasgow school", and still evidenced the strong influence of the Arts & Crafts movement. In 1900, after his designs had already become clearer and more geometric, Mackintosh participated in an exhibition of the Viennese Secession,

and inspired numerous Viennese architects to seek a reduced formal idiom.
In 1902, he was commissioned to build a residence for the family of a Glasgow publisher. The result was an architecture that to some extent was reminiscent of traditional manor houses with their turrets, oriels, and gabled roofs, but at the same time embodied a very modern, Cubist, reduced view of things. The transition between the living room and bedroom - one of the few rooms that Mackintosh designed in its entirety - features an open fireplace. Everything contained in the bedroom, including the fixtures, is painted white. He finally abandoned the last traces of the curved Art Nouveau ornamentation when creating the frugal designs for the bed, cupboards and carpets, and instead employed grid-like, often square symbols that reveal strong Japanese influences.
Two black chairs were firmly placed in an alcove to create striking contrasts to the overall composition. Thanks to their extra-tall back-rests with the typical square pattern at the upper end, these objects radiate a calm, almost meditative energy. However, their refined construction would hardly have withstood constant use. Mackintosh was less concerned here with function than with creating an effect.
This formed the real difference between his ideas and the Arts & Crafts movement or the Viennese representatives of Art Nouveau, for whom longevity and sound construction based on good craftsmanship took precedence. By showing that a chair need not be defined by its utility value, but instead can possess an artistic

value independent of functional considerations, Mackintosh paved the way for numerous 20th century designers with his chair design for the Hill House. MK

10

Name:	**Westport Chair**
Designer:	**Thomas Lee**
Draft:	**1903**
Production:	**around 1904-30**
Manufacturer:	**Harry C. Bunnel, Westport, New York**
Measurements:	**H 105; W 98; D 95 seat height 40/26 cms**
Materials:	**varnished wood**

The Westport Chair was inspired by an armchair which Thomas Lee designed in 1903 for his bungalow in Westport, New York. Lee took simple wooden boards, such as those used for garden bowers or crates, and with them fashioned the most comfortable and stable chair possible, with wide arm-rests that also functioned as proper rests. A friend of his, cabinetmaker Harry C. Bunnel, began producing the Westport Chair in 1904, and shortly afterwards had it patented. Bunnel produced the model with minor changes through 1930, and, in addition, devised a sofa, a rocking chair and a children's chair all based on the design.

As the chair was easy for people to assemble at home, it soon became highly popular in all circles. During the 1920s, the Westport Chair served as the model for the Adirondack Chair, a lesser dimensioned garden chair that became the hallmark of American front yards and bungalows. However, with its slatted back-rest it differed from the Westport Chair, which always used a solid board.

The similarity between the Westport Chair and the Roodblauwe Stoel, designed 15 years later by Dutchman Gerrit Rietveld, is astonishing. However, there is nothing to suggest that Gerrit Rietveld could have known of this chair. The Westport Chair, also known as "Uncle Tom's Chair", was the work of an amateur, and was never marketed on an international scale. It is speculated that the first examples of this chair arrived in Europe in 1923, in other words five years after Rietveld's design. While Roodblauwe Stoel went down in design history as a milestone, the Westport Chair has only in recent years been acknowledged as a collector's item. MK

11

Name:	**Chair No. 511**
Designer:	**(firm draft)**
Draft:	**1905**
Production:	**from 1905**
Manufacturer:	**Gebr. Thonet, Vienna**
Measurements:	**H 99.5; W 42; D 50 cms**
Materials:	**bent beechwood, molded Plywood**

With their low-priced, industrially manufactured furniture, Thonet endeavored to reach as broad a swath of buyers as possible. While Thonet only used anonymous factory designs, their rivals Jakob & Josef Kohn started, as of about 1900, to manufacture furniture designs by Viennese architects, and were increasingly successful with these first "designer" products. Thonet thereupon also expanded their sales line to include furniture which exhibited the stylistic elements of the architects' designs while mixing these with Art Nouveau forms.

One example is chair No. 511 dating from 1905; its underlying construction is borrowed from Art Nouveau. The dynamic sweep of the bentwood section, which continues from the front legs, curving upward to form the back-rest, is clearly reminiscent of drafts by Richard Riemerschmid, a German, or those of Frenchman Gaillard. No. 511 has also been associated with the aesthetics of Henry van de Velde. However, whereas van de Velde or Riemerschmid, like almost all representatives of Art Nouveau, strove to create organically shaped, sculptural forms of furniture (and this often involved costly craftsmanship), the No. 511 chair was already manufactured entirely using industrial processes.

This was possible thanks to the use of simple squared timber, which had, in turn, first been used by the Viennese architects for furniture. The sparse use of ornamentation on the back-rest also brings this latter group to mind: their geometric, formally reduced designs were the diametrical opposite of Art Nouveau furniture designs.

The problems of such an eclectic approach are revealed by the somewhat awkward solution for constructing the back legs, which had to be strengthened by means of inserted supports. This also indicates that the No. 511 was hardly the structurally and stylistically demanding work of a designer, but rather a pleasing (indeed highly successful) item of mass furniture. MK

12

Name:	**No. 728, Fledermaus, (Chair for the Cabaret-Café Fledermaus)**
Designer:	**Josef Hoffmann**
Draft:	**approx. 1905**
Production:	**approx. from 1905 to 1920**
Manufacturer:	**J. & J. Kohn, Vienna**
Measurements:	**H 72; W 55; D 49 cms**
Materials:	**bent beechwood, lathe-turned beechwood, bent laminated wood**

At the turn of the century, the cabaret-cum-café Fledermaus in Vienna was the meeting place for the Viennese Secession, a group founded in 1897 by artists from all fields who wished to break with the reactionary, strictly academic artistic tradition of the 19th century. Architects such as Josef Hoffmann, Kolomann Moser, Otto Wagner or Gustav Siegel were among the members of this influential circle. Aiming to forge a link between art and craftsmanship, they worked with craftsmen to produce furniture or everyday objects that clearly depart from the curved floral designs of the Art Nouveau movement. These more geometrical objects did justice to the materials used, and, in combination with the buildings designed by the same group, formed interiors that transcended the ostentatious feel so preferred in the 19th century. With such objects, the group exerted a significant influence on modern interior design. After

metal that had previously been used to reinforce this joint.

Adolf Loos had created his influential design for Café Museum in 1897, designing the interior of cafés and other prominent public spaces in particular became an alluring opportunity for the proponents of the Viennese Secession.

In creating the Cabaret-Café Fledermaus in 1905, Josef Hoffmann painted the walls in radiant colours that contrasted strongly with the black-and-white checked tile floor. Hoffmann made use of this strict black-and-white scheme for the chairs, with white chairs ornamented with black balls, and the black chairs with white balls. The basic unpainted version of these models first appeared as No.728 in the 1905 catalogues of the J. & J. Kohn company.

Hoffmann's straightforward yet clever construction for the so-called Fledermaus Chair is a compromise between a highly stylized aesthetics and the requirements of cost-effective series production. The back-rest, seat and base ring all follow the same horseshoe curve, and are linked via the back legs, which in turn have the same cross-section as the front legs.

Thanks to the circular base, the construction can withstand a high degree of lateral stress despite its light weight, and could be assembled quickly using a few elements that were easy to produce.

Finally, the spherical connectors between the legs with the seat - the trademark of Hoffmann's designs - were more than just decorative elements. Instead, they replaced the curved or angular braces made of wood or

Because it was used in Cabaret-Café Fledermaus, the chair became a model for numerous similar versions that were produced by different furniture companies as of 1907. MK

13

Name:	**No. 670 , Sitzmaschine**
Designer:	**Josef Hoffmann**
Draft:	**about 1905**
Production:	**c. 1905-16**
Manufacturer:	**Jacob & Josef Kohn, Vienna**
Measurements:	**H 106; W 67.5; D 90; seat height 35 cms**
Materials:	**bent beechwood, turned wood, plywood, brass**

This type of easy chair with a reclining back has been produced since the seventeenth century. After 1860 the company owned by Englishman William Morris, founder of the Arts and Crafts movement, manufactured and marketed this chair. With its stringent, no-frills design focusing only on elementary parts, it probably served as a model for the later designs of Josef Hoffmann.
The Arts and Crafts movement, which greatly influenced Hoffmann and his colleagues Gustav Siegel and Koloman Moser in Austria, was opposed to mechanized mass production and what they regarded as inhuman products. The movement advocated an ethic and aesthetic motivated by social concerns, with form, function, material, and production understood as a unity. Around the turn of the century the Jacob & Josef Kohn company, which produced bentwood furniture to an industrial standard, hired the avant-garde Viennese architects Hoffmann, Siegel and Moser to make their line more appealing to higher-end clients by means of

fashionable designs.
Hoffmann's model No. 670 was presented as part of one of his most important projects, a furnished model country home for the Vienna Art Show in 1908. The chair was distributed by Jacob & Josef Kohn until 1916. Here, the admittedly pedestrian form of the reclining easy chair is given a striking mechanical look. The frame construction made of bent squared timber with a frame filled with geometrically arranged pieces of plywood and the semi-circular curves of the rear section emphasize the constructive aspect of the object. The balls which are as functional as they are decorative - a typical detail of Hoffmann's - balance the curved and rectangular elements. At the same time as they stabilize the chair in the corners of the structure and under the runners, they support a shiftable crossbar on the rear arches which locks the back section at different reclining angles. Additionally, they create a visual balance to the square holes in the side and back sections.
Presumably Jacob & Josef Kohn also offered an upholstered version of the Sitzmaschine, as the model No. 670 was later called. The example shown here with a pull-out footrest was probably a special order. MSC

14

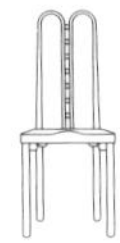

Name:	**No. 371**
Designer:	**Josef Hoffmann**
Draft:	**1905/06**
Production:	**c. 1906-1910**
Manufacturer:	**Jakob & Josef Kohn, Vienna**
Measurements:	**H 109.5; W 44; D 50.5; seat height 47 cms**
Materials:	**bent and turned beech wood, formed plywood**

Like his Sitzmaschine, this chair was designed by Josef Hoffmann for a country house, presented at the Vienna Art Show in 1908.

The chair stands out above all for its bold back, reminiscent of an upright spine. It emerges from the sturdy back legs which narrow as they move upward and form two slender high arches containing seven balls in the central axle. The chair was frequently called the "Seven Ball Chair" as a consequence, and the balls are repeated in the angles between seat and chair legs. Here they have not only a decorative but also a constructive function, as they stabilize the joints. The saddle-shaped plywood seat offers a pleasant supporting surface and its rounded form with an upward thrust blends optically with the sturdy base.

The motif of the balls framed in the bentwood struts was probably first used as a decorative wall frieze, when in 1901/02 Jacob & Josef Kohn presented some of the company's interior designs at the Winter Exhibition of the Austrian Museum for Art and Industry. Evidently, this prefigured the coming schism and the turn away from the symbolist trend of the Viennese Secession, going instead toward a geometric idiom borrowed from architecture. With the craftsmanship orientation of the Wiener Werkstätten, which Hoffmann with the architect Koloman Moser and the banker Fritz Wärndorfer founded in 1903, any allusions to the floral Art Nouveau disappeared from his work. MSC

15

Name:	**Armchair No. 721 (Armchair for the Viennese Post Savings Bank)**
Designer:	**Otto Wagner**
Draft:	**1905/06**
Production:	**as of 1905**
Manufacturer:	**J. & J. Kohn, Vienna**
Measurements:	**H 80; W 54.5; D 56.5 cms**
Materials:	**bent beech and bent plywood**

During his years as a professor at the Vienna College of Arts and Crafts, Otto Wagner taught a number of illustrious pupils, including Josef Hoffmann and Josef Maria Olbricht. He was already a renowned architect and teacher when, in 1900, he joined the Viennese Secession, a group of artists wishing to turn their backs on the artistic tradition that had prevailed in the late 19th century. Wagner was commissioned to design both the buildings and the interior of the new Viennese Post Savings Bank, which was constructed between 1904 and 1906. He was the first representative of the Secession to be entrusted with such an important public project.
Wagner's architecture did not rigidly adhere to the principles of functionalism, but instead sought to reveal functional aspects through aesthetics. Nonetheless, he had a great impact on modern architecture with this building, in particular with the design for the main hall. Wagner not only had the columns of the hall clad with

aluminium, in those days a novel material, he also added clearly visible ornamental studs in many places, and arranged rows of unconcealed heat vents along the walls. The ceiling is completely covered with opalescent glass, and the load-bearing elements for it are not visible from the inside, so that the hall is bathed in a uniform light.
One of the items which Wagner designed for the interior furnishings was an armchair, produced in different versions for the smaller offices right through to the management level. The form of the chair was based on a design by Gustav Siegel, presented by J. & J. Kohn at the Paris World Fair in 1900. Siegel had been the first to bend squared timber, whereas previously this technique had only been applied to round sections of wood. A single piece of bentwood was used to create the curved back-rest as well as the front legs and the armrests - another innovative feature of this model's construction.
Otto Wagner had already modified Siegel's design in 1902 to furnish "Die Zeit", the dispatch office in Vienna. He dispensed with the upholstery in Siegel's model, and brought together the separate leg supports to form a single base ring. In addition, he added metal braces to the arm-rests and feet, but these were only superficially functional, as they did not extend to the edges of the wood, the places that were actually subject to stress.
In designing the chairs for the Post Savings Bank, Wagner merely made a few alterations to his own 1902 design. He only reinforced the inside curves of the two back legs and replaced the board supporting the backrest with two cross struts. However, he produced

different versions to correspond with the different tiers in the bank's hierarchy. Thus, a modest version was designed for lower-level employees, with no metal braces and canework covering. The armchair intended for staff higher up featured wood or leather seats. The next versions up the scale featured green or yellow velour upholstery; like all the models, these were fitted with low base cuffs, with or without metal fittings on the arm-rests. The director's chair was covered with red velour and sported high brass base cuffs, but no arm-rest fittings. MK

16

Name: **Robie House Chair**
Designer: **Frank Lloyd Wright**
Draft: **1908**
Production: **1908**
Manufacturer: **F. H. Bresler Co., Milwaukee**
Measurements: **H 133; W 43.2, D 50.2 cms**
Materials: **oakwood, leather**

Frank Lloyd Wright, whose creative career spanned almost seven decades - from around 1890 to 1959 - was one of the most influential architects and designers of the 20th century. After completing an apprenticeship in the studio of architect Louis H. Sullivan, he started working independently in 1893. Wright developed an architectural concept intended to create a harmony between the various elements involved, in which the building, the furniture and objects followed the same overarching design principles. He consequently insisted on designing most of the interiors of his own buildings.
Between 1902 and 1909, he designed a series of buildings known as the Prairie Houses, a name which refers to the spacious approach and an interior layout inspired by the experience of North American vastness. With these buildings, Wright developed a new kind of residence and coined the term "organic architecture" to describe it, one of the most important currents in modern architecture.
The Robie House was erected in 1908 in Chicago, and embodies the main features of the Prairie Houses. On

the exterior, the horizontal plane pre-dominates in the long, ship-like house. Frank Lloyd Wright's geometric idiom, in part inspired by Japanese motifs, surfaces in all aspects of the interior design - the square motif, rhomboid grid patterns, and crystalline and round forms. Living and dining room take up an entire floor, and are separated only by a large, central fireplace.
The dining room was dominated by a heavy dining table featuring wood fixtures with glass lamps and bowls for flower arrangements at all four corners. Six chairs were grouped around this table. With their conspicuous, protruding back-rests, similar to the designs by British designer Charles Rennie Mackintosh, they imply that the user must adopt a strict, straight posture. The seat, legs and back-rest have been reduced to the basic forms. The squared timbers of the back-rest, arranged vertically, extend all the way down the back legs as a stabilizing element, so that only two low cross struts suffice to reinforce the legs. As with most of the designs he created for clients, Frank Lloyd Wright had the high-grade furniture for Robie House made from solid oak wood by specialist craftsmen.
Both Wright and Mackintosh had already developed a chair with a high back-rest in around 1895, and used it for the interior design of their buildings, although there were major stylistic differences between the two. Wright first used his chairs to furnish his own house in Oak Park, Illinois, in 1895. There, the characteristic long back-rest slats up as far as the seat, while the two sturdier side elements featured lathe-turned ornamentation at their upper ends. Until 1910, Wright designed numerous

other chairs with extra-long back-rests, including the model shown here, which stands out on account of its clarity and simplicity.

However, the general feeling of austerity connected with the entire dining group in the Robie House made it seem more appropriate for a ceremonial feast than a relaxed family meal. As a result, it was reserved for festive occasions, whereas the family took its regular meals at a smaller table - also sitting on chairs designed by Frank Lloyd Wright. MK

17

Name:	**-**
Designer:	**Vlastislav Hofman**
Draft:	**1911/12**
Production:	**1911/12**
Manufacturer:	**Prazské umelecké dílny, Prague**
Measurements:	**H 90; W 43; D 46 cms**
Materials:	**black stained oak, veneered, leather upholstery, brass upholstering nails**

Around 1907, Cubism emerged in Paris, a style which is considered to be the first high point of modern abstract painting. In their early Cubist works, artists such as Picasso or Braque dissected their subjects into rectilinear, crystalline shapes and thus created an independent world alongside that of naturalistic perception. Some three years later, numerous architects and artists in Prague adopted the still nascent Cubist outlook and applied it to architecture and design. An active movement emerged between 1910 and 1920, known today as Czech Cubism. It rejected the traditional, artificial ornamentation, and also the rationalist principles of Viennese Modernity. The cubist forms in architecture and design had a dynamics of their own, and were intended to render ornamentation superfluous; indeed, they appear to break the laws of physics.

Vlastislav Hofman, an architect, designer, painter and

stage-set designer, was one of the main proponents of this movement. Like the Cubist painters, he was fascinated by the art of primitive tribes in Africa, and attempted to adhere to their straightforwardness and expressive power in his works. "The new art uses means that are as striking and expressive as possible, and thus also most abstract in terms of form.(...) The basic form arises from the inner qualities of the matter (conception of the movement of the matter)."
The chair which Hofman designed for the dining room of the sculptor Maratka is a visual statement on the same theme. The pyramid-shaped legs, the back-rest - reduced to a symbolic sign - and the massive proportions lend the furniture the decidedly raw plasticity of an African sculpture. Unlike other designs produced by Czech Cubism, which tend to be more dynamic, Hofman's chair impresses the viewer with its well-balanced form, interrupted only by an arrow-like relief on the rear of the back-rest. Together with a formally-related armchair, the chair contrasts with the otherwise conventional decor of the dining room.
While other representatives of Czech Cubism created only unique pieces or commissioned work, Vlastislav Hofman had this and other designs produced by the Künstlerische Werkstätte in Prague as a mini-series. When Czech Cubism was later honored during the Eighties as a unique, inspiring stylistic phenomenon, Hofman's chair design was again produced in small numbers. MK

18

Name:	**Roodblauwe Stoel**
Designer:	**Gerrit Thomas Rietveld**
Draft:	**1918**
Production:	**since 1918**
Manufacturer:	**Gerard van de Groenekan, Utrecht**
Measurements:	**H 86; W 66; D 82.5; seat height 32 cms**
Materials:	**varnished wood**

Gerrit Rietveld conceived of each piece of furniture as an ideal, abstract composition of surfaces and lines in space. The rigor with which he put this into practice makes "Roodblauwe stoel" a key object in modern furniture design.

The form of abstraction Rietveld adopts here bears comparison to painter Piet Mondrian. Mondrian, and later Rietveld, were among the artists and architects who grouped around Theo van Doesburg and his journal De Stijl, and whose radical concepts had a lasting impact on twentieth-century art. Both Mondrian and Rietveld reduced given realities to their linear and surface characteristics: where Mondrian took landscapes as his model, Rietveld focused on the concept of a traditional, massive armchair, which he transformed into a geometric entity. In doing so, as Rietveld himself explains, he was concerned with joining "the components without crippling them, so that to the greatest degree possible the one is not dominated or made dependent on the other; most importantly, the work in its entirety must be able to stand freely and brightly on its own two feet, and the form must triumph over the material."

The followers of De Stijl adopted the Roodblauwe Stoel, at that point still in its first, unpainted version, as their manifesto. It was the initial object which served to illustrate the principles of the group to the public at large, and provided Theo van Doesburg with an outstanding example of furniture as "abstract, realistic sculptures for our future interiors."

However, Rietveld's own remarks raise doubts as to whether he, like van Doesburg, actually claimed to be pursuing the social utopia of universal harmony. He apparently did not believe that his furniture could contribute to causing universal social change, and built it primarily for himself and his private acquaintances. As a result, there is no specific prototype of the chair, only a number of variations which have relatively little in common. As Reyer Kras, curator of the Stedelijk Museum in Amsterdam, writes, Rietveld was evidently conscious of the fact "that formal order has nothing to do with precalculated, strictly repeated sizes and proportions, but rather is exclusively the domain of a good eye." However, Rietveld felt it should in principle be possible to produce his chair on an industrial scale. The elements used were excellently suited both for self-assembly furniture and for mass production, as they could be manufactured with the simplest mechanical means and were already available as standardized wood lengths.

The first version of the Roodblauwe Stoel, still unpainted and somewhat larger than the later model, as well as having side panels under the armrests, was built by Rietveld around 1918, in other words shortly before he joined De Stijl. The well-known version — from which the design took its final name — with its red back, blue seat, and yellow front on black struts, first appeared alongside different-colored variations around 1923, when Rietveld already belonged to the inner circle of the group. The differentiation of the colors on the surfaces further underscores the contrast between the abstract form and the material quality of the furniture. The Italian company Cassina has been manufacturing this version of the chair since 1973. MSC

Wright
Rietveld
Breuer
Stam
Van der Rohe
Rasch
Le Corbusier
Jeanneret
Perriand
Herbst

3

1921-1930

The Breakthrough of Modernism

An economic boom a few years after World War I led in the large European and American metropolises to an optimistic outlook and pulsating life. The cityscape started to be shaped by gigantic office buildings and department stores, cars and streetcars. Even before the war, artists and intellectuals had joined together to form numerous avant-garde groups, and now **Modernism** broke through in full force. In their pictures, painters like Wassily Kandinsky, Piet Mondrian or Casimir Malevich expounded the first principles of **abstract art**; its conception of space was soon to be paralleled in architecture and the applied arts.

The **De Stijl** movement which grew up as of 1917 around **Theo van Doesburg**, and of which architect **Gerrit Rietveld** (18, 20, 25, 38, 39) was also a member, combined strict **rationalism** with a spiritual, almost mystical conception of art. Space and surface are reduced in the works of the De Stijl group to strictly rectangular compositions, and the preferred colors were the primary colors yellow, red and blue. Gerrit Rietveld put this concept impressively into practice in his **Roodblauwe Stoel** (1918-24), and also in his architecture, such as the **"Schröder House"**, built in 1924.

One of the most important centers of the artistic **avant-garde** in the 1920s was the **Bauhaus**, founded by **Walter Gropius** in Weimar in 1919. Although initially still influenced by the theories of the De Stijl movement, it geared itself increasingly toward practical work and its social meaning. Architects, craftsmen, painters, sculptors and numerous visiting lecturers worked closely together in the Bauhaus, developing ideas which shaped the face of Modernism. In all areas of the applied arts, they searched to combine a reduced, **functionalist approach to design** with human needs in an epoch defined by industry and technology, for which the word **machine age** was then coined.

Important steps in this direction were **Marcel Breuer's** (21, 26, 31, 36) 1925 designs for the first **tubular steel** household furniture and **Ludwig Mies van der Rohe's** (23, 32, 33) 1927 cantilever chair, the first of its kind.

Since tubular steel is ideally suited for the mass production of furniture, and its cool, hygienic appearance jelled with the avant-garde's view of furniture that did justice to the age, this material within a very short time became the most popular material used by designers and architects alike.

In France, **Le Corbusier** (27, 28, 29), **René Herbst** (30) or **Eileen Gray** were among the most influential champions of Modernism. Their tubular steel furniture stood out for the fact that it nevertheless still used upholstery; and in the works of **Pierre Chareau** we can still sense links to **Art Déco**, which dominated the France of the day.

Russia, since the October Revolution in 1918 the first country under communist rule, was a further center of avant-garde art. In Moscow, a group of artists called for a radically abstract and dynamic approach to design,

something that has gone down in the annals of history as **Constructivism** and **Suprematism**.
Many members of these movements regarded **communism** as an opportunity to bring their ideas of industrial production to bear in a collective society. MK

19

Name:	**Peacock Chair (Chair for the Imperial Hotel)**
Designer:	**Frank Lloyd Wright**
Draft:	**1921/22**
Production:	**unknown**
Manufacturer:	**unknown Japanese company**
Measurements:	**H 96; W 38; D 50; seat height 44 cms**
Materials:	**oak, oil cloth covering, metal**

The interior design of a house, and the fitted or movable furniture in it, up to and including lamps and even musical instruments, had a fixed place in the architecture of Frank Lloyd Wright. He regarded this as the ornamental extension of his buildings, just as he believed the buildings were abstractions and organic extensions of their environment.
His work foregrounded a Constructivist aesthetics, whereby an internal harmony of freedom and calmness was meant to pervade the outer form. To his mind, the unity of a city, a house, or an item of furniture depended on the integration of its parts, and each form had at the same time to reflect its origin. Wright believed that ornamentation was an essential expression of creative imagination, which produces "natural patterns to structure itself."
He designed the Peacock Chair, with its complicated

and concentrated ornamentation, in his draft for the Imperial Hotel in Tokyo, which was built between 1915 and 1922 - in terms of ground plan, elevation, and decoration the building is considered one of his most complex works. The hexagons in the back and on the sides of the chair's base are also encountered in numerous places in the building: in the ceilings, on walls, and even in a coffee set designed by Wright. Since the chairs were quite fragile, they were changed at least three times in the life of the hotel, which was torn down in 1968. The presumably earliest models had wickerwork instead of upholstery on the seat and backs as well as in the hexagons on the sides. MSC

20

Name: **Militaire Stoel**
Designer: **Gerrit Rietveld**
Draft: **1923**
Production: **as of 1923**
Manufacturers: **G. van de Groenekan, Utrecht**
Measurements: **H 89.5; W 41; D 52 cms; seat height 44.5 cms**
Materials: **varnished wood and plywood**

Gerrit Rietveld is one of those designers who had a decisive influence on 20th century architecture and design. His Roodblauwe Stoel from 1918 is regarded as one of the most important works of modern furniture design.

In 1923, Rietveld was commissioned to design furniture for the interior of the Catholic Military Academy in Utrecht. Unlike the Roodblauwe Stoel and other previous experimental furniture designs, the contract called less for a programmatic statement on chairs and more for stability, lightness and the lowest possible production costs.

It is thus no surprise that the design for the military academy chair involves a simple construction. The back-rest is attached to the back legs which run right up the back of the chair; the legs are reinforced with simple cross struts, and support the seat. The design underscores the chair's open construction, which had become Rietveld's trademark following Roodblauwe

Stoel. Instead of having seat and bearing frame meet flush, Rietveld staggered the legs and cross struts, allowing them to protrude beyond the seat. However, the construction shown here was not realized with the same degree of consistency as his more artistic Roodblauwe Stoel. For reasons of stability, the struts had to be joined using grooves. Furthermore, they are fastened with clearly visible screws, while the completely separate elements of Roodblauwe Stoel are fastened by almost invisible rawlplugs. However, the screws enabled the Militaire Stoel to be assembled on location, and dismantled if necessary.
Because the workshop run by Rietveld's partner, G. van de Groenekan, was unable to produce the number of chairs required to furnish the Military Academy at short notice, he gave the order to another manufacturer. This first series most likely received a coat of green varnish. In the time that followed, G. van de Groenekan produced imitations of the Militaire Stoel in different colours for his private customers; these later versions all more or less corresponded to the original. Rietveld also used a red version of the Militaire Stoel for the kitchen of his best known building, the Schröder House, erected in 1924. MK

21

Name: **Armchair B 3, Wassily**
Designer: **Marcel Breuer**
Draft: **1925**
Production: **1926/27**
Manufacturer: **Standard Möbel Lengyel**
Measurements: **H 72.5, W 76.5; D 69.5; seat height 43 cms**
Materials: **cold bent, nickel-plated tubular steel; polished-yarn fabric**

Steel tubing was first used for hospital furniture as of about 1890, for car seats by Czech manufacturer Tatra starting in 1919, and for airplane seats in the Fokker plants as of 1924. It was first introduced to home furnishings with Breuer's steel club armchair, which marked an aesthetic turning point in furniture production as well as the start of an important branch of industry. Although the chair was not a direct product of the Bauhaus workshops, its history is a perfect example of the spirit underlying this influential institution. For Bauhaus followers, industrial production was " the most modern means of design," as Walter Gropius, the founder of Bauhaus, wrote in 1923 - and thus its economic and aesthetic model. The choice of material and construction clearly place B 3 in an industrial context that Breuer expected would lend living a more functional aspect: "This metal furniture is to be nothing more than a

necessary device for modern-day living."
Breuer's enthusiasm with the stability of his newly procured Adler bicycle gave him the idea of using tubular steel to make furniture. At that time, he was the director of the Bauhaus wood workshop in Dessau. He first turned to the bicycle manufacturer in 1925 in the hope of realizing his idea. However, Adler was not interested in furniture production. He then commissioned Mannesmann, the company which had developed the seamless cold-draw process for tubular steel in 1885/86, to bend the necessary components into the proper shape. Subsequently, he employed the services of a plumber and collaborated with him in building the first prototypes. In the same year - perhaps a historical coincidence - Le Corbusier presented a staircase made of tubular steel in the "Pavillon de l'Esprit Nouveau" in Paris, a staircase that was built "like a bicycle frame."
The most important innovation of Breuer's design lay in reducing the basic design of a heavy club armchair to a light frame made of welded steel tubes. The "B 3" also reveals the influence that Gerrit Rietveld's furniture had on Marcel Breuer's Bauhaus designs, as the position of the seat and backrest clearly evokes Rietveld's Roodblauwe Stoel. To a far greater extent than with wood structures, the reflective nickel-plated surfaces of the steel tubes rendered the construction transparent, an effect further enhanced by reducing the surfaces to thin lengths of fabric. Breuer's ideal, which he formulated in a film from 1926, was to make sitters think they were sitting on "springy

columns of air." The taut material prevents the user from coming in contact with the cold steel parts of the complex frame, and, in addition, forms an appealing contrast to the metal. In deciding upon the upholstery, which was to mirror the shine of the tubular steel, Breuer first considered a horsehair weave, which proved to be too expensive and too complicated to work with. Furthermore, he discovered that it was unstable, as the loops around the steel tubes broke easily. Finally, so-called "Eisengarn" was developed in keeping with Breuer's concept. This material was used in many subsequent designs, such as the B 35.

In what is presumably the first version, known only from a photograph, the welded frame of the tubular steel chair had four separate legs and the backrest was shaped like an upright U. The next version was sold as the B 3 by Standard Möbel, a company founded by Breuer, Kálmán Lengyel, and Anton Lorenz in 1926 to market Breuer's designs. The first B3 consisted of nine separate welded parts. The seat and back were separate units in a frame consisting of an endless loop of tubular steel, in which both pairs of legs were joined together to form parallel runners that served as the base. Breuer had most likely discovered this motif in the nearby Junker airplane factory, where the runners of the worktables enabled them to be pushed aside more easily. Standard Möbel then made additional changes to the design: to start, the components of the construction were no longer welded, but instead were held together with

screws, nuts, and slot-in connectors. The back was no longer made of a U-shaped tube, but was now constructed of two separate L-shaped side pieces attached to the seat with screws.
When taken apart, more than fifty chairs can be stored in a crate measuring just one cubic meter, even more than Thonet's legendary model No. 14. In a later stage of development, the back was stabilized by bringing together the side pieces to form an arch at the top. In 1929 Standard Möbel was bought by Thonet, which kept B 3 in its program for only two years, but during that time made even further changes: both runners were braced with a straight cross-strut, and instead of the connector located in front of the seat, which interfered with the sitter's legs, a bent cross strut that ran under the upholstery was used to strengthen the seat frame. In 1962 production was relaunched by the Italian company Gavina, which was later acquired by Knoll. In honor of Bauhaus master Wassily Kandinsky, who from early on had called attention to the revolutionary aesthetics of the chair, Gavina dubbed it "Wassily," as it is popularly known today.
Initially B 3 only caught the admiring attention of architects, designers, artists, and visitors at the Bauhaus in Dessau, where it stood in a number of homes in the master's settlement. At Breuer's 1926 solo exhibition at the Kunsthalle in Dresden, the chair was already being acclaimed as a masterpiece. Breuer's fascination for space-saving collapsible furniture also led him to design a folding version of

the B 3 in 1926, and he obtained the German patent for both models in 1927. Along with the tubular steel furniture that had meanwhile been produced by Mart Stam, Mies van der Rohe, and others, Breuer presented his chair at the prestigious exhibit "Die Wohnung" (the apartment) in Stuttgart. For the first time, industry and the public at large were able to feast their eyes on the B 3. People quickly learned to appreciate tubular steel furniture due to its lightness, hygienic qualities, and resistance to wear-and-tear. In the thirties, it even became a fashion in its own right, and today is the epitome of the spirit of Modernity in the first half of the twentieth-century. MSC

22

Name:	**Chair W1**
Designer:	**Mart Stam**
Draft:	**1926**
Production:	**1927**
Manufacturers:	**L. & C. Arnold**
Measurements:	**H 83.5; W 45.5; D 53.5 cms**
Materials:	**varnished tubular steel, fabric belts**

In 1925, architect Marcel Breuer created the first modern chair made of tubular steel - his B 3 armchair. However, despite the use of this modern material, the production method relied on traditional methods for working wood - the individual elements of the armchair were screwed together. Only after the invention of the so-called cantilevered chair, which had no back legs, did designers take advantage of the characteristics specific to tubular steel.
Dutch designer Mart Stam produced the first prototypes for such a cantilevered chair in 1926, using sawed-off gas pipes which he linked with elbow butting. The base frame, legs, seat and back-rest were created by a continuous loop bent at right angles. At a preliminary meeting for the construction of the Weissenhof Settlement in Stuttgart, Stam explained his design to architect Ludwig Mies van der Rohe, among others. Van der Rohe recognized the importance of Stam's idea and began to develop his own cantilevered chair, as he considered Stam's version to be unsatisfactory. In 1927,

both Stam and Mies van der Rohe presented a cantilevered tubular steel chair at the Weissenhof Settlement. In the meantime, Stam had had his design produced by the L. & C. Arnold company, which also featured it in their sales program for a year. Unlike the prototype, the Arnold chair was made from a single piece of tubular steel with a diameter of just 20 mm, and with walls 2 mm thick. The bends in the tube had to be reinforced with solid iron rods, and thus lacked any springiness. The chair was painted black or gray, and, with its covering of rubber or coarse fabric, had a rather unassuming appearance.

Mies van der Rohe's design, on the other hand, featured a base loop that was connected to the seat with an elegant semicircle; furthermore, the steel tube had a diameter of 25 mm and was chrome-plated. The larger diameter afforded a crucial advantage: the chair required no internal reinforcement, and in addition it was springy, so that Mies was able to have it patented as the first "cantilevered chair", independent of Stam.

The presentation of both chairs heralded the commercial breakthrough of tubular steel furniture. Numerous furniture companies now commissioned architects and designers to design chairs based on the cantilever principle. A legal battle ensued between the owner of the rights to Stam's design, Anton Lorenz, and the Gebr. Thonet company, whose sales model was very similar to that of Stam. In 1932, Stam was finally awarded the artistic copyright for the cantilevered chair made of steel bent at right angles, after a verdict passed by the Reich's Court certified his design as the "embodiment of modern

realism with the most simple means in the most reduced form". Further protracted legal battles over the cantilevered chair illustrate its commercial significance.
Although his idea was commercialized by the furniture industry, Mart Stam always focused first and foremost on social issues. As a sworn pragmatist, he saw his invention merely as a means of producing and selling chairs at low cost. Indifferent to the aesthetic aspects of tubular steel, he stuck with the construction of the prototype for his original cantilever chair in later designs as well because assembling short pieces of tubular steel produced less waste than forming elegant constructions from a single tube. MK

23

Name:	**MR 20**
Designer:	**Ludwig Mies van der Rohe**
Draft:	**1927**
Production:	**1927-1930**
Manufacturer:	**Berliner Metallgewerbe Josef Müller, Berlin**
Measurements:	**H 79.5; W 46.5; D 71; seat height 40 cms**
Materials:	**nickel-plated tubular steel, ron wool**

As vice president of the Deutscher Werkbund from 1926-1932, Mies van der Rohe was familiar with the realization of the overall Weissenhof Settlement project near Stuttgart when the Werkbund exhibition opened there in 1927.

In the course of the preparations he met with Heinz Rasch, Mart Stam, and others in Stuttgart on November 22, 1926. During this meeting, Mart Stam explained his design of a chair without back legs and sketched the same. Since Stam was interested in a cubist, geometrically stringent look, he chose to use lengths of gas piping which were screwed to each other with angle fittings with small radii. Mies came back from Stuttgart and talked to his employees about Mart Stam and his idea for the chair. "We had a drawing board on the wall on which Mies drew the Stam chair, as right angles from top to bottom. He even added the sockets and said: 'Ugly, these sockets are so ugly. If he had only rounded them off - that would have been much more attractive' and sketched a curve. - The single curve he drew on the Stam sketch gave birth to the new chair." Several Stam chairs were manufactured in the Eisenmöbelfabrik Arnold in Schorndorf near Stuttgart for the interior of a Stam house in the Weissenhof Settlement, but without any sockets of hot-molded iron piping. As the sockets were too soft, the first prototype Stam sat on gave way under his weight. Reinforcements of round iron inserts created a sufficiently stable yet resilient structure.

Meanwhile, Mies van der Rohe was experimenting with Mannesmann precision tubular steel, which he bent cold to retain the elastic quality of the thin-walled tubular steel. The semicircular curves of the front legs enhance this effect, since they optimally support the springy function of the tubing.

Just after Mart Stam, Mies van der Rohe also exhibited his chairs, the first cantilever-based chairs in the Weissenhof Settlement. The flexibility of the structure afforded the same seating comfort otherwise only afforded by upholstered chairs and armchairs, without any of their associated coziness. The delicate lightness of the tubular steel furniture predestined them for the interiors of the New Building movement.

In the year of their launch, Mies van der Rohe also applied for a patent for the cantilever in the United States. His application was at first turned down with reference to the American patent Harry E. Nolan had taken out in 1924 (applied for in 1922) which already planned a cantilever-based garden armchair with spiral springs. Only after Mies van der Rohe was able to prove

that this solid chair made of steel round rods could never be springy - he built a prototype for the model, which was never produced - did he receive the patent. A wave of adaptations, improvements and also curios in tubular steel soon appeared as a reaction to the Werkbund exhibition in the Weissenhof Settlement.
Today, Mies van der Rohe's cantilever-based chair is marketed in different versions by Tecta, Thonet and Knoll International. PD

24

Name: **Sitzgeiststuhl**
Designer: **Heinz and Bodo Rasch**
Draft: **1927**
Production: **1927**
Manufacturers: **Heinz & Bodo Rasch, Stuttgart**
Measurements: **H 88; W 43; D 50 cms**
Materials: **plywood, black varnish**

From 1920 to 1923, Heinz Rasch studied architecture in Hanover and Stuttgart while from 1922 to 1926 his brother Bodo first completed studies in agriculture and then took on an apprenticeship as a joiner. In 1922, in other words while students, the brothers founded the "Werkstätte zur Herstellung von Einrichtungsgegenständen" in Stuttgart and regularly presented their chair designs at Deutscher Werkbund exhibitions in Stuttgart between 1924 and 1928.
In 1928, the Rasch brothers brought the experiences they had acquired as furniture designers in working with constructions, ergonomics and anatomy to bear in the form of a book entitled "Der Stuhl". In this educational tome, they systematically presented the most important types of chairs and, with the help of their own designs, substantiated their claim that a chair designer must follow only functional and ergonomic criteria. "The chair serves to ease the burden on the body.(...) Earlier, there were 100 different types of chairs to meet 100 different seating needs. To satisfy the demand for one chair for

100 needs (...) - no doubt a precondition for perfect industrial production - one would have to create a universal chair which could comply with every individual need."

At the 1927 Werkbund exhibition in Stuttgart, the Rasch brothers caused a sensation with the presentation of their Sitzgeiststuhl. In "Der Stuhl", they explain how its unusual construction was derived from the form of a human body frozen in a knee-bend. This posture is visualized by the flat wooden side frames, into which the back-rest, the seat and the two supporting "leg" surfaces are inserted. It is made of flat plywood boards and, as explained in "Der Stuhl", is a simplified version of a squared timber construction. The solid sash angles of the frame give the chair a soft look throughout, and replace the corner struts used in traditional chairs. Reinforcing the chair vertically, in other words in the direction of stress, enabled them to use a single base with a sufficiently large footprint in place of legs.

The cantilevered tubular steel chair, which was developed at around the same time, stemmed from a context unlike that of Heinz and Bodo Rasch's Sitzgeiststuhl, however when viewing both from the sides certain parallels can be drawn. As with the cantilevered chair, the slender profile of the frame at the legs and in the back-rest even enables the user to bounce gently.

The Rasch brothers recommended the Sitzgeiststuhl in particular for public transportation on account of its springiness. However, there were few buyers, and in the end the chair was produced in small quantities by "Werkstätte zur Herstellung von Einrichtungsgegenständen". Yet the Sitzgeiststuhl is repeatedly honored, albeit belatedly, as the purported model for the Zig-Zag Chair of 1934, a design classic by Dutch designer Gerrit Rietveld. MK

25

Name:	**Beugel Stoel**
Designer:	**Gerrit Rietveld**
Draft:	**1927**
Production:	**as of 1930**
Manufacturer:	**Metz & Co., Amsterdam**
Measurements:	**H 92; W 61; D 88 cms**
Materials:	**varnished tubular steel, varnished plywood**

Architect and furniture designer Gerrit Rietveld was a central figure in the avant-garde movement of the 1920s. However, unlike many other innovative designers, he was less interested in a particular aesthetics than in discovering uses for new materials and structures. As early as 1927, he was the first designer to try to produce a chair from a single piece of a given material using folding and inserting techniques. The design for the Beugel Stoel also aimed at minimizing the number of components in order to guarantee low-cost production and easy transport.
As with most of his experimental designs, Rietveld had the first prototypes produced in the workshops of Gerard van de Groenekan. The panel used for the seat and backrest was made of vulcanized fibers. It was bent into the desired shape and affixed to two solid iron side supports that resembled runners. Initially, the ends of the iron rods were not welded, but instead crossed beneath the seat, where they were bolted together. At both ends, the seat and backrest followed the curves of

the supports, reinforcing the construction against lateral stress and rendering cross struts superfluous.
The prototypes for the Beugel Stoel produced in van de Groenekan's workshop were shown in 1928 at the Stuttgart exhibition entitled Der Stuhl, where their intelligent construction was greatly admired. Even at this early date, Rietveld was able to present different versions of the chair with varying seat and backrest heights, or with armrests. Numerous contemporary publications reveal that Beugel Stoel was thought to be the first design in which seat and backrest were a single structural element that had been formed from a single panel. Today, we know that there are isolated examples of chairs produced using this technique that date back to the 19th century.
Around 1930, the Amsterdam furniture store Metz & Co. included several models of the Beugel Stoel in its collection. In collaboration with Rietveld, Metz made various alterations to the design and began producing the chair in larger quantities. The heavy yet brittle vulcanized fibre seats were replaced with lighter bent plywood boards, imported in large quantities from Scandinavia. The side supports were now made of welded tubular steel instead of iron, reducing the weight considerably, so that the chair was actually as light as it looked. The Beugel Stoel was Rietveld's first experimental design suitable for series production, and thus reached a broader public. MK

26

Name:	**B 64, Cesca**
Designer:	**Marcel Breuer**
Design:	**1928**
Production:	**1929 to the present**
Manufacturer:	**Gebrüder Thonet AG, Frankenberg**
Size:	**H 81 W 57 D 62.5; seat height 45 cms**
Materials:	**chrome-plated tubular steel, varnished wood, bentwood, wicker**

Marcel Breuer's cantilever-based chair is one of the best-known chairs in the world, but it often first came to the attention of consumers as a cheap imitation. Breuer's fondness for tubular steel and his knowledge of how to use it in chair construction was already illustrated in the club chair B 3 introduced in 1925.
Breuer was revolutionary in abandoning the traditional construction of a chair based on four legs, but he was not the originator of this idea. The Dutch architect Mart Stam had already introduced the notion of a cantilevered chair to Heinz Rasch and Ludwig Mies van der Rohe in 1926 during the preparation of the Werkbund exhibition "Die Wohnung" (the apartment) for the Weissenhof Settlement in Stuttgart. The design was a far cry from a free-swinger for it was rigid. Ludwig Mies van der Rohe was the first to pick up on the idea of a chair without back legs with his models MR 10 and MR

20 and continued the straight barrel shape in a single curve to the seat. Both chairs were presented in the exhibition "Die Wohnung" in 1927 where Marcel Breuer saw them.

Although Breuer allowed many of his tubular steel designs to be produced as standard furniture, he gave the production rights for the B 32 (without armrests) and the B 64 to Thonet.

Stam's complaint about the use of his designs was rejected by Breuer with the argument that he had already designed a U-shaped stool in 1925/26 for the canteen of the Bauhaus which - if it were laid on its side - anticipated the principle of the cantilevered chair. The main difference from Stam's model lay in the combination of tubular steel construction with wooden frames for the seat and back, with a bentwood technique referring to the origins of the bending of tubular steel.

Even if Breuer was not the originator of the cantilevered chair, his springy free-swinger became his greatest commercial success.

When the Italian company Gavina s.p.a. took over production of the Breuer designs in 1962, the B 64 received the nickname "Cesca" after Breuer's adopted daughter, Francesca. PD

27

Name:	**B 302, Siège tournant**
Designers:	**Le Corbusier, Pierre Jeanneret, Charlotte Perriand**
Draft:	**1928**
Production:	**1929 - 1935**
Manufacturers	**Le Corbusier, Pierre Jeanneret, Charlotte Perriand, Paris**
Measurements:	**H 72 W 63 D 55, seat heigth 30 cms**
Materials:	**tubular steel, leather and foam upholstery**

At the Paris Autumn Salon in 1929, Le Corbusier, Pierre Jeanneret and Charlotte Perriand - designers and architects - presented a series of furniture in an interior entitled "L'équipement d'une habitation". Here, they united an avant-garde aesthetics of tubular steel furniture with a preference for a distinctive and comfortable design such as was especially distinctive in French Art Déco.

Some of the furniture had already been used prior to its public presentation in 1929; for example, the swivel tubular steel armchair, which Charlotte Perriand (a staff member in Le Corbusier's office since 1927) had created in the spring of 1928 for a dining room suite she presented at the "Salon des Artistes Décorateurs". The chair is an original variant on the bentwood office chairs that had been produced since the mid-19th century and which had quickly become popular. Swivel chairs crop up at an early date in catalogs of tubular steel furniture: thus, we find a design by Marcel Breuer in a Standard Möbel catalogue of 1927. While Breuer's draft, with its small wooden seat, is a plain working chair, Le Corbusier, Jeanneret and Perriand created the same type of chair but with lush upholstery and great aesthetic appeal. They foregrounded less the economic aspects of tubular steel and more the semantics of the furniture in the context of architecture and interior design. In this way, they stressed functionality in what was customarily a comfortable domain, using the Siège tournant in their installations as a dining chair and thus taking it out of its original context.

The chair's construction is however not completely functionally defined. The frame, the massive upholstered seat and the back-rest , all clearly separated from one another in shape, are joined as if by abrupt collage. Especially the original, hose-like back-rest creates an eye-catcher, lending the chair an expression similar to the ready-mades by Marcel Duchamps and the dadaists which appeared at roughly the same time.

Like the similarly constructed back-less stool and other Le Corbusier designs, Siège tournant was manufactured by Thonet Frères. The armchair and stool were produced as B 302 and B 304 until approx. 1935 and thus survived the longest of all Le Corbusier, Jeanneret and Perriand furniture in the Thonet line. In a brochure brought out in approx. 1930, a chair version B 303 is shown, which seems almost absurd, since here the

upholstery-hose from the back-rest of the B 304 is reduced to a short stump and only fastened in the middle of the seat.
In addition to the mass produced version, there is also a slightly varied, early model of the Siège tournant, with armrests which are not rectangularly positioned at the lower end, but like an arch merge with the seat.
Since the 1960s, Cassina has created a re-edition of the furniture designed by Le Corbusier, Jeanneret and Perriand. MK

28

Name:	**B 301, Fauteuil à dossier basculant**
Designer:	**Le Corbusier, Pierre Jeanneret, Charlotte Perriand**
Draft:	**1928**
Production:	**c. 1928 (before series production)**
Manufacturer:	**Le Corbusier, Pierre Jeanneret, Charlotte Perriand, Paris**
Measurements:	**H 64; W 64; D 67; seat height 39 cms**
Materials:	**chrome-plated tubular steel, leather, steel springs**

Le Corbusier always chose pieces of furniture with an intelligent structure and timeless design for the sparse and functional furnishing of his houses, such as a so-called "colonial chair" by the English firm, Maple & Co. "Indian Chair No. 1761" seems to have served as model for the design shown here but also convinced Le Corbusier, Pierre Jeanneret and Charlotte Perriand of the necessity of creating a more comfortable furniture. One important common feature is the back section, which can be tilted by two side attachments and thus supports the back in any position. The idea for this design was being developed in the Le Corbusier studio at just about the same time as the designer Eileen Gray created her Transat chair for the house E-1027. What was new about the chair by Le Corbusier, Jeanneret, and Perriand, however, was the translation of a customary basic form into an elegant piece of tubular steel furniture which emphasized the functionality of the simple tilting mechanism. Instead of straight tubes to attach the seat and to mount the back section on the legs, the back is pushed forward and supported together with the seat by a single connector which is welded from one straight and one bent tube. The complicated form intentionally departs from the right angles of the rest of the construction to emphasize the comfort of the chair, the reclined seat, and the mobile back. The back section in the early version shown here revolved freely around the central axis; later the rear suspension for the armrests was extended inwards so that the back was only partly moveable. In addition to a leather covering, the chair was also available in patterned calfskin for the back and seat. The earliest models, including one in calfskin, were produced for the library of the villa Church in Ville d'Avray in 1928 by craftsmen under Charlotte Perriand's supervision. Other models were exhibited during the 1929 Paris autumn salon at the "L'équipement d'une habitation" stand created by Le Corbusier, Pierre Jeanneret, and Charlotte Perriand. The plan was for the Peugeot company to mass-produce the Siège à dossier basculant, along with other furniture designed by this architect team, as that firm was already experienced in processing tubular steel for the construction of bicycles. However, the plan did not materialize, and the Thonet Company was approached to handle the costly production of a version that was almost identical as of 1930, the model B 301. Afterward it was manufactured by the Swiss Embru Company under license from Thonet, then by Heidi Weber, and from 1965 to the present by Cassina. MSC

29

Name:	**B 306, Chaise longue à reglage continu**
Designers:	**Le Corbusier, Pierre Jeanneret, Charlotte Perriand**
Draft:	**1928**
Production:	**since 1930**
Manufacturer:	**Thonet Frères, Paris**
Measurements:	**H 70; W 56.6; D 156 cms**
Materials:	**chrome-plated and varnished steel, fabric, steel springs, rubber**

Compared to the social ideas of the Bauhaus and its minimal designs, French tubular steel furniture, which was influenced by Art Deco, could be considered luxurious. The extravagant shapes and combinations of materials corresponded to the needs of Parisian society for a decidedly modern quality of life and comfort.
The few furniture designs which Le Corbusier and Pierre Jeanneret sketched in cooperation with Charlotte Perriand included different drawings of chaises longues. However, not a single item had ever been realized; except for a few bookcases which, however, must be classified more as a permanent fixture of the open, spacious buildings that Le Corbusier furnished in a technical, functional manner and conceived of as "living machines. His approach called for sparse and functionally related furnishing, e.g., like Thonet's

armchair No. 6009, the modernness of which was rediscovered through its predominant use in Le Corbusier interiors. Charlotte Perriand, whose nickel-plated copper furniture had just been introduced at the 1927 Paris autumn salon, joined the studio Le Corbusier shared with his cousin Pierre Jeanneret at the end of that year. Between 1928 and 1929, presumably to a great extent based on Le Corbusier's sketches, the three created different pieces of furniture such as a swivel stool, tables, armchairs, and a chaise longue. Included among these designs, which are all highly regarded today, is this chaise longue which is undoubtedly one of the most famous items of twentieth-century furniture. In 1928, in a perspective interior view, Le Corbusier sketched the chaise longue which consists of a padded surface bended sharply twice and resting on the edge of the foot section, supported at the head by a column. In newspaper advertisements of the same year, the Paris physician Pascaud publicized an anatomically shaped lounge chair with an adjustable back piece and neckrest, the so-called "Surrepos." Surely Le Corbusier was also familiar with a rocking chaise longue, equipped with an adjustable back: Thonet's Rocking Sofa No. 7500. But Le Corbusier, Jeanneret, and Perriand did not wait until the "Surrepos" was on the market and approached the idea from an entirely new perspective. They designed a multifunctional structure which made the reclining surface, fixed on a pair of bows, independent of the base. Since this section rests loosely on the H-shaped supports of the base, its inclination can be adjusted continuously. The rubber sleeves around the crossbeam

of the support prevent slipping when someone uses the chaise longue. When the reclining surface is lifted off the base, the bows serve as runners for a rocking recliner.
The different parts of this chaise longue also visually communicate the dynamic of its versatility, even with regard to such details as the inclination of the H-shaped supports, whose oval, crosssections are similar to the wings of an airplane. (They were tear-shaped in the original model.) Le Corbusier, who was fascinated by the aesthetics of machines, also called this chaise longue a "relaxing machine."
In the first model, which was produced by craftsmen under the supervision of Charlotte Perriand for a library of the villa Church in 1928, the ends at the foot and head sections of the chair were still welded on and thus interrupted the continuous line of the tubular steel frame. An example of this type of chair was exhibited by Le Corbusier, Jeanneret, and Perriand at their "L'équipement d'une habitation" stand at the 1929 Paris autumn salon. In the next model, designed for the gallery in the villa La Roche in 1928, this formal inconsistency was corrected. The original scale drawings of this model, which the three designers passed on to Thonet, coincide with the contract signed in 1929 and formed the basis for production, which began in 1930. The example shown here was probably a Thonet prototype. The elliptical profile of the bar between the front and back sections of the base is already like those used in the Thonet mass-produced versions. Unlike here, in the original as well as with the mass-produced design, the front and back sections of the base were at the same

height. Thonet advertised this piece of furniture in a 1930 catalogue with a canvas or calfskin covering. In the meantime the chaise longue was produced again by the Swiss Embru Company under license from Thonet and from 1965 until the present by Cassina. MSC

30

Name: **Chaise sandows**
Designer: **René Herbst**
Draft: **1928-9**
Production: **since 1929**
Manufacturer: **Etablissements René Herbst, Paris**
Measurements: **H 81.5; W 46.5; D 44.5; seat height 46 cms**
Materials: **varnished tubular steel, rubber stretcher belt (expander)**

René Herbst is considered one of the first designers in France to use tubular steel for furniture construction. His most important furniture designs using this material were made between 1927 and 1937. In addition to tubular steel, he also worked with new materials such as rubber, Bakelite, and plastic.
René Herbst explained that he believed the most important criterion in designing an armchair was that it could stand on four feet and look as simple as possible. Thus, the armchair belonged to a series of seating whose designs were characterized by simple, clear lines and offered great sitting comfort with a minimum of material.
The seat and back sections were made of elastic rubber stretcher belts (sandow in French) which were known from expanders. Herbst was accordingly the first person to introduce the motif of the objet trouvé into furniture

design.
The belts are hooked onto the frame of the chair, a type of connection that is also reminiscent of an expander.
The chair's transparency and adaptability to body contours predates fifties design methods. The visible structural work and the purity of the lines are essential elements in the timeless designs of René Herbst. PD

31

Name:	**Armchair B 35**
Designer:	**Marcel Breuer**
Draft:	**1928/29**
Production:	**c. 1930 to the present**
Manufacturer:	**Gebrüder Thonet AG, Frankenberg/Eder, Germany**
Measurements:	**H 82.5; W 60; D 80; seat height 35 cms**
Materials:	**chrome-plated tubular steel, iron wool, varnished wood**

Marcel Breuer is widely recognized as one of the most important furniture designers of the twentieth century. In 1930, following an undeniably successful period as head of the Bauhaus furniture workshop in Dessau between 1925 to 1928, together with Walter Gropius and Herbert Bayer he set up the section for the Deutscher Werkbund as a part of an exhibition of the French Society of Decorative Artists in the Paris Grand Palais. At this much acclaimed premiere of German design in France following World War I, he for the first time presented his club chair "B 35," which he had designed in 1928/29.
With this ingenious design, Breuer succeeded in integrating all the functions of a cantilever tubular steel chair into the structure of a single continuous line. This afforded an extremely comfortable doubling of the cantilever effect, because the armrests, which swung

independently of the seat, balance the bounce of the seat and back frame which canitevers toward the back; in addition they pleasantly give way when leaned upon while standing up or sitting down. The steel tubing, which runs from the armrests through to the runners and then shapes the seat and back, actually consists of three parts which are joined and screwed together beneath the covering sewn around them. Making the many bends in a single piece of continuous tubing might have been technically possible at that time but would still have been very complicated. Crossbars in the front and back as well as a spreader bar under the seat offer greater stability.
Breuer combined the technical coolness of tubular steel with wooden armrests and iron wool for covering the seat and back. The exact positioning of these elements ensures that the user does not come in contact with the cold steel. Iron wool is a stiff cotton fiber which glistens like metal due to treatment with wax. The fiber was developed in 1926 at the Bauhaus in Dessau specifically for covering Breuer chairs after the horsehair fiber which was originally used proved to be too expensive and insufficiently resilient.
The first known version of the B 35, for a Berlin town apartment, was upholstered; the 1930 version exhibited in the Grand Palais was covered in leather. From 1930-1937 Thonet produced the chair with leather, iron wool, or wicker coverings and from 1971 to the present with leather or wicker. The position and the type of attachment for the crossbars already varied in the first models. MSC

32

Name: MR 90, Barcelona Chair
Designer: Ludwig Mies van der Rohe
Draft: 1929
Production: 1929/30
Manufacturer: Berliner Metallgewerbe Josef Müller, Berlin
Measurements: H 75; W 76; D 77; seat height 43 cms
Materials: chrome-plated steel strip, leather belts, leather cushions

Mies van der Rohe designed the German pavilion and corresponding furniture for the 1929 world's fair in Barcelona. Among other things, his pavilion served as the setting for the inaugural ceremony led by the Spanish royal couple, Alfonso XIII and Victoria Eugenia.

While Mies van der Rohe implemented his ideas of avant-garde steel and glass architecture for the building design, he drew his inspiration for the furniture from historic models.

Mies van der Rohe took as his starting point the ancient, scissors-shaped collapsible folding chair, already a symbol of power among Egyptian rulers. In ancient Greece, this chair represented the throne used by gods and mortal rulers alike, and in the Roman empire served as a magistrate's chair (sella curulis). It had been manufactured in various cultures - in particular on the Iberian peninsula - through to modern times, although it has lost its previous importance. It owed this popularity to its clever folding mechanism, variations of which gave rise to the deck chairs found on large oceanliners at the beginning of the century.

In keeping with the occasion, Mies van der Rohe adopts the representative qualities of the scissors chair, although he does without the folding function and interprets it afresh.

In order to match the overall impression of luxury in the pavilion, evoked by wall panels made of onyx and marble, as well as delicate, chrome-plated steel supports and stained glass of various colors, Mies van der Rohe chose not to use wood like the historic models, but instead employed chrome-plated steel strip and white leather upholstery with button stitching. Despite the use of different materials, various features in the construction of the first series bring to mind the model made of wood.

While the gently curved pieces of strip steel that form the sides were generously welded at the intersections, the right and left sides were joined with steel transverse braces of equal diameter. These were mounted with screws, using the "square corner halving process" employed in wood-frame construction.

Subsequently, this form of assembly was shifted from the corners to the interior of the frame, as the screws could be hidden there behind the leather straps. A number of variations on the joints from this early production phase are known, all of which were extremely costly. In 1948 they were finally replaced by a frame that was welded throughout. At the same time, the volume of the welded points of intersection on the sides was reduced, lowering the need for regrinding and polishing of the welds. Finally, as of 1964, the chrome-plated steel strip was replaced with polished high-grade steel.

A feature common to all variations is the weave of the leather upholstery, which evokes the alternating cross pattern of the slats used in the wood chairs.

Interior photographs of the Tugendhat house in Brno, Czech Republic, built a year after the Barcelona pavilion, already show variations on the frame with different numbers of straps, for example the version with square corner halving shown here. This feature classifies it as belonging to the first batch produced by Berliner Metallgewerbe Josef Müller in Berlin.

The pavilion was torn down after the fair. However, along with the furniture, it was retrospectively acknowledged as a showcase for the International Style that had taken hold throughout the world.

The Barcelona pavilion was reconstructed and rebuilt in 1986. PD

33

Name:	**MR 50, Brno Armchair**
Designers:	**Ludwig Mies van der Rohe**
Draft:	**1929**
Production:	**1929**
Manufacturers:	**J. Müller, Bamberg Metallwerkstätten, Berlin**
Measurements:	**H 79.5 cm; W 58 cm; D 58 cms**
Materials:	**flat steel, chrome-plated, hide covering**

In 1928, Ludwig Mies van der Rohe was commissioned by Grete and Fritz Tugendhat to design a villa for them to be located above the city of Brno (in the Czech Republic). When the house was completed in 1930, it provoked great excitement, not least thanks to an enthusiastic newspaper article by the clients themselves. In Villa Tugendhat, Mies van der Rohe brought to bear in a private residence his open spatial concept and the luxurious atmosphere which had already distinguished the Barcelona pavilion he had created in 1929. Cruciform columns form the load-bearing elements in the skeleton construction, enabling Mies van der Rohe to arrange the living space using vacant, non-bearing walls made of onyx marble and ebony. One long glass facade in the living and dining room incorporates the outside world into the architecture and creates a generous sense of space.

Originally, Mies van der Rohe had wished to furnish Villa

Tugendhat with the furniture he had drafted in 1926 for the Weissenhof Settlement in Stuttgart. Since these were, however, too large and overly curved backwards, (for example, in order to surround a dinner table), van der Rohe designed a cantilever-based chair with smaller dimension than the Weissenhof furniture; with its upholstery, it has a more elegant look than its predecessors. The contrast between the tense sweep of the steel frame and the right angles of the seat and back-rest, fastened to the frame in an almost invisible manner, gives the so-called Brno chair a particular charm of its own.

For Villa Tugendhat, the chair was manufactured both of chrome-plated tubular steel as well as from flat steel and covered with white or red leather.

As series-produced furniture, the chair was produced as early as 1929/30 by J. Müller in Berlin. In 1930/31, the company was renamed Bamberg Metallwerkstätten and published a brochure containing all of van der Rohe's seating furniture and offering the Brno chair as model MR 50 in chrome-plated, nickel-coated or varnished flat-steel versions, alternatively with fabric, leather or parchment covers. After Thonet bought the company, production was discontinued at the beginning of the 1930s. When, in 1960, Knoll launched its re-edition of the flat-steel version, followed in 1977 by the tubular steel version, a hide cover was also offered.

In addition to this model, Mies van der Rohe drafted a chair for Villa Tugendhat which in terms of dimensions and its loose upholstery is reminiscent of the chair for the Barcelona pavilion. The construction of the base-frame allows the seat to swing free. Like the Brno chair, the chair combines the main issue in furniture design in the 1920s, namely the cantilever base, with Mies van der Rohe's typical elegance. MK

The miniature concentrates, like tomato sauce, the essence and the full flavour of the project.

Michele De Lucchi, Designer, 1997

Aalto
Luckhardt
Breuer
Summers
Rietveld
Terragni
Prouvé
André
Coray
Grupo Austral

4

1931-1940

The Avant-Garde, Styling, Repression

In 1928, a dramatic stock exchange crash brought the economic boom of the 1920s to a sudden end and triggered a world economic crisis. In Europe and the United States, the number of unemployed rocketed, governments were no longer able to absorb the consequences of rampant capitalism. In Russia, Germany, Italy and Spain the **economic crisis** forms the seedbed for **totalitarian regimes**, which often managed to control all areas of the state, including art and design, only shortly after taking over at the helm. In Italy, the fascist government took the stage as the promoter of Modernist architecture and design (40). The **futurist** movement, which glorifies technical progress, was also swiftly gobbled up by fascism.
After seizing power in 1933, the **Nazis** in Germany were far more inconsiderate. Overnight, many artistic innovations of the 1920s were declared to be **"degenerate"**. The Bauhaus was closed in 1933 and all the important lecturers such as **Walter Gropius**, **Marcel Breuer** (21, 26, 31, 36) or **Mart Stam** (22) had to flee into **exile**. The Nazis propagated a petty-bourgeois, uniform home decor, while public buildings were meant to embody the omnipotence of the party by means of a historicizing, pathos-laden architecture.
In the struggle to combat the impact of the economic crisis, the offensive was taken in the United States to boost industrial and agricultural activity. The government

created new jobs by means of major public construction commissions. In the process, design was recognized as an instrument with which to favorably influence **marketing** and thus the economic success of a product. Based on this insight, the first design studios arise, which concern themselves with **industrial design** with a view to market strategy.
The search for appealing **styling** helped promote the spread of so-called **streamlined design** (37). Originally developed to enhance the **aerodynamics** of vehicles, ships and airplanes, this form soon influenced even the design of simple household appliances. Among other things, the dynamically and organically shaped parts started to be manufactured using the first plastic technology and other new processes. The gleaming **chrome** of cars, technical instruments and furniture reflects the mechanized culture of a comfortable life at the pinnacle of progress.
Tubular steel furniture, initially still the province of a small, interested public, has become a mass-produced article. In the wake of the fundamental innovations achieved by the avant-garde in the 1920s, many designers deepened their experiments and now started to apply them to mass production. While **Jean Prouvé** (43) made use of ultra-modern aircraft construction technique in his architecture and his furniture designs, **Marcel Breuer, Gerrit Rietveld** (18, 20, 25, 38, 39) or **Jacques André** (43) use new materials such as **aluminum** and **acrylic glass** in their creative work. The manufacture of adjustable, **ergonomic seating** becomes an important branch of industry.(41)

At this time, Finnish architect and furniture designer **Alvar Aalto** made important progress in the area of shaping wood laminates. Proceeding from a rationalist approach, he designed furniture from two-dimensionally molded wood laminates, with a shape that was organic and emphasized clean lines.

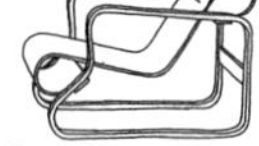

34

Name:	**Armchair No. 41, Paimio**
Designer:	**Alvar Aalto**
Draft:	**1930/31**
Production:	**1932 to the present**
Manufacturer:	**Oy. Huonekalu-ja Rakennustyötehdas AB, Turku, Finland for Artek Oy. AB, Helsinki**
Measurements:	**H 62.5, W 61, D 88; seat height 34 cms**
Materials:	**bent plywood, bent laminated birch wood frame**

In 1928 Alvar Aalto and his wife Aino won the architectural competition to build a tuberculosis sanitarium near the Finnish city of Paimio; construction had just begun (1929-1933) when they were also commissioned to do the building's interior design. They initially considered using the new Bauhaus tubular steel furniture - they already owned the B 3 club chair designed by Marcel Breuer - but then quickly decided in favor of wood, "for much of this nickel and chrome-plated steel furniture seemed to us to be psychologically too hard for an environment of sick persons. We thus began working with wood, using this warmer and more supple material in combination with practical structures to create an appropriate furnishing style for patients".

The first examples of these attempts were shown 1929 at the 700th anniversary celebration of the city of Turku. In 1933 work on the Paimio sanitarium was completed, and at the suggestion of Architectural Review, Aalto's architectural projects and furniture designs were shown in the London department store Fortnum and Mason's. The following year, the new furniture was already a part of the standard program at Wohnbedarf AG in Zurich.
As the manufacturer's export marketing left much to be desired, Alvar and Aino Aalto opened their own gallery and distributing company in 1935, inspired by Wohnbedarf AG in Zurich. The enterprise, which they called Artek was to be a "center for contemporary furniture, interior decoration, art and industrial art." Aalto soon enjoyed worldwide fame after presentations at the VI Milan Triennial in 1936, and having designed the Finnish pavilion for the 1937 world's fair in Paris and the 1939 world's fair in New York, preceded by a solo exhibition of his work at the MoMA in 1938.
The "Paimio" chair quickly became popular and was produced in large quantities. It is made of bent laminated veneer and is the result of numerous bending trials using birch wood that is in part naturally damp. As birch wood is plentiful throughout Finland and the production method required no expensive technology, it was possible to manufacture the chair at relatively low cost. Despite its lack of upholstery, the springy seat afforded comfortable sitting, and was suited for modern interiors with its

contemporary, natural, and unobtrusive form. It paved the way for the Scandinavian-influence furniture design which lasted until the sixties. PD

35

Name:	**ST 14**
Designers:	**Hans and Wassili Luckhardt**
Design:	**1931**
Production:	**1931**
Manufacturer:	**Desta (Deutsche Stahlmöbel), Berlin**
Measurements:	**H 87.5; W 53.5; D 61; seat height 44 cms**
Materials:	**chrome-plated tubular steel, molded and varnished plywood**

Hans and Wassili Luckhardt belonged, as did the Taut brothers, Hans Scharoun, Ludwig Mies van der Rohe, and Walter Gropius, to a group of young architects who met with the established architects Hans Poelzig and Peter Behrens after World War I in Berlin and Dessau. In this circle visionary, socially critical ideas were exchanged; artistically these men felt an affinity to Expressionism and Cubism. The architect, they believed, should be a creative protagonist in redesigning society. While these ideas later found a Rationalist expression in the Bauhaus, the work of the Luckhardt brothers always suggested a freer attitude toward form which Wassili Luckhardt described in the year 1921: "Putting aside pencil and ruler, I take clay and plasticine and begin to knead directly and without outside influences."
With this approach, the Luckhardt brothers also took advantage of the qualities of tubular steel for building

furniture. The unusually elegant shape of the cantilever-based ST 14 which was produced from 1931 on by the Desta Company, extends far beyond the geometrical, Cubist forms of the Bauhaus school to achieve a streamlined aesthetic. In contrast to Mies van der Rohe's cantilevered MR 10, with its curves in precise semi- and quarter-circles, the tubular steel here is bent into an organically flowing line. The back is completely adapted to the rounding of the tubular steel and the seat appears to float freely in the form. The chair comes close to the aesthetic ideal of tubular steel furniture as Hans Luckhardt formulated it in 1931: "The quiet, attractively taut line predominates."

Hans Luckhardt compared the stylistic influence of tubular steel in furniture making with the influence of the skeletal steel manner of building high-rises, Luckhardt's main interest in the latter half of the twenties. At the 1928 "Home and Technology" exhibition in Munich, they presented a miniature flat built in a skeletal steel manner and outfitted with tubular steel furniture.

After the beginning of 1931, the Luckhardt brothers had a stake of RM 0.60 per unit in the sales of their models under a license agreement with Anton Lorenz, the founder of Desta. In the so-called Desta-Haus at the 1931 Berlin Building Exhibition, they put the ST 14 on show, which was also available with a seat that could be flipped up.

When Thonet took over the Desta company in 1932, only those chairs still in stock were taken on. In 1984 Thonet relaunched production of the ST 14. MK

36

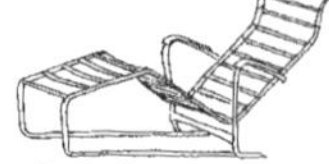

Name:	**Chaise longue No. 313**
Designer:	**Marcel Breuer**
Draft:	**1932**
Production:	**since 1934**
Manufacturer:	**Embru AG (Eisen- und Metallbettenfabrik AG, Rüti) for Wohnbedarf AG, Zurich**
Measurements:	**H 75.5; W 58; D 137 cms**
Materials:	**aluminum "Anticorodal" alloy, varnished wood**

The Chaise longue No. 313, part of a collection of different springy aluminum chairs and recliners, is the product of two different developments.

Marcel Breuer, who emigrated from Dessau to Zurich, had already applied to the National Patent Office for the German patent for a "frame for springy chairs or recliners" on November 22, 1932. A lawsuit ensued which continued for a year between the companies of Mauser (Cologne) and Arnold (Schorndorf) and Mies van der Rohe, until finally on September 10, 1936, the patent application was turned down. The point at issue was the copyright for the rigid connection of the (rear) so-called "auxiliary spring supports" which, by relieving the burden, enabled a reduction in the tube diameter. At the end of 1932, Marcel Breuer directed the modernization of a new shop in Talstrasse 11 for Wohnbedarf AG in Zurich, which had been founded in

1931 by, among others, the architectural critic, Sigfried Giedeon. The goal of Wohnbedarf AG was to develop, more or less as a distributer, contemporary furniture with a light appearance for apartments made in the New Building style - in cooperation with designers and the industry.

When the Alliance Aluminium Cie. announced the competition "Concours international du meilleur siège en aluminium" in Paris in 1933, Giedeon succeeded in establishing a second jury, parallel to that of industry representatives, with artistically oriented members, such as representatives of CIAM (Les Congrès Internationaux d'Architecture Moderne). As CIAM secretary, Giedeon also made his colleagues Le Corbusier and Walter Gropius members of the jury.

Marcel Breuer participated in the competition, submitting prototypes of springy chairs and recliners made of aluminum which he had had produced by Embru. He was awarded first prize on November 23 and 24 by two juries that had reached their decisions independently of each other. The intelligent construction principle was quite striking, with a symmetrical aluminum section sawed lengthwise and then bent to form both the front and the back auxiliary spring supports.

Earlier, on October 21, 1933, Breuer had signed a license agreement with Embru for the exclusive production and sales rights, initially for Switzerland and Liechtenstein, and had applied for a Swiss patent on October 31, 1933. This application was more or less equivalent to the previously rejected Berlin patent but was expanded to include solid materials, such as wood and metal. A patent was granted on November 1, 1934, by the Swiss Office for Intellectual Property after Embru had already begun mass production, also in lacquered strip steel. Other license partners for the springy "Anticorodal" or "Duralumin" series included Arnold in Germany, A. L. Colombo in Italy, and Stylclair in France.

The designs in the aluminum series met with great popular acclaim and formed the link between the tubular steel furniture of Breuer's days at the Bauhaus in Germany and the plywood furniture which he developed during his emigration to England between 1935 and 1937. PD

37

Name:	**(Plywood Armchair)**
Designer:	**Gerald Summers**
Draft:	**1933/34**
Production:	**since 1935**
Manufacturer:	**Makers of Simple Furniture, Ltd., London**
Measurements:	**H 67.4; W 60.5; D 91.5; seat height 32 cms**
Materials:	**bent plywood**

In the history of industrial design there have always been attempts to shape everyday objects in only one piece of semifinished industrial material like rods, tubing, wire, or sheets. There is hardly a design that better illustrates the ideal unity of material, production and form, however, than this armchair by Gerald Summers. His admirably simple construction dispenses with connectors and almost with off-cuts, using one single sheet of plywood. Following a simple pattern, Summers separated the back legs from the back and armrests and bent the segments thus created in different directions. The result was an organically shaped armchair, comfortable even without cushions, involving low material and labor inputs.
Possibly the chair was conceived for use in the tropics. With its smooth surface and lack of metal connectors, it is hygienic and deteriorates only gradually. Its unusual shape probably stems from Alvar Aalto's furniture, especially the spectacular Paimio chair, which was shown in London in 1933. In his own company, Makers of

Simple Furniture, Ltd., founded in 1929, Summers produced only 120 units of the chair. Despite the constructive advantages, the production costs of the chair and thus the sales price were higher than the designs of the popular Scandinavian. It was certainly also a disadvantage that the back legs could not withstand great stress and snapped easily. MSC

38

Name:	**Zig-Zag Stoel**
Designer:	**Gerrit Thomas Rietveld**
Draft:	**1932**
Production:	**1935 to c. 1955**
Manufacturers:	**Metz & Co., Amsterdam**
Measurements:	**H 75; W 37; D 44.5; seat height 42.5 cms**
Materials:	**red-stained elm, brass screws**

As a variation on the model of a chair without back legs first developed by Mart Stam, Gerrit Rietveld's Zig-Zag chair remains one of the most radical formulations in furniture design. Presumably the immediate forerunner was Heinz and Bodo Rasch's eye-catching Sitzgeiststuhl (sitting spirit chair) of 1927. Its shape, which the Rasch brothers fashioned to match the posture of a person sitting, consisted of a base and a curved surface bent twice for the back and the upper and lower thighs. Comparable to tendons in human limbs, the construction of the rounded side sections is thus stabilized. Rietveld abstracts from the quite complicated but structurally correct form to create a simple zigzag, but the logic of the construction suffers. Actually a whole series of tests were necessary to achieve a practical solution. Zig-Zag appears to completely contradict our ideas of a usable piece of furniture since its free-standing surfaces appear to collapse as soon as any weight is placed on them. However the chair is stabilized by dovetail joints between

the seat and back, reinforcements with screws and nuts, as well as wooden wedges in the corners. Rietveld was very much aware of the discrepancy between the simple shape and the relatively complicated construction and said himself, it is not a chair but a "designer joke."
The actual goal of the design was to create a functional form which does not displace space but allows it to be perceived as a continuum; indeed, of Rietveld's entire body of work the Zig-Zag represents the most economical example of such a form. It is an uncompromising transposition of minimal requirements onto a chair, reduced to such an extent that even the screws appear to be decorative.
An idea that always accompanied the history of furniture design - of mechanically producing a chair out from a single continuous form - led Rietveld to his first experiments with bent, spliced plywood in 1927. In 1932 he began designing what later became the so-called Zig-Zag chair for the Amsterdam furniture manufacturer, Metz & Co. Plywood or chip wood on a metal frame was a failure, however. Not until 1934 did he succeed in creating a stable, very comfortable, and even stackable version. From 1935 this was produced with somewhat differing proportions, connections, and surface treatments by both Rietveld's master cabinetmaker and Metz & Co., in great numbers up until the fifties. The model shown here stems from such a production in the thirties. The producer of today's version of the Zig-Zag is the Cassina Company which purchased the rights to manufacture all of Rietveld's furniture designs in 1971.
Rietveld used the Zig-Zag together with a matching table

in many of his later interiors and also created an armchair version with and without a perforated back, as well as a Zig-Zag children's highchair. MSC

39

Name:	**Krat Stoel**
Designer:	**Gerrit Rietveld**
Draft:	**1934**
Production:	**1934 to approx. 1955**
Manufacturers:	**Metz & Co., Amsterdam**
Measurements:	**H 60.5; W 57.5; D 77.5; seat height 27 cms**
Materials:	**pine, white wood varnish**

In 1934, Gerrit Rietveld, a furniture designer and architect, resorted to an unusual method to build furniture: he took untreated, coarse planks for crates and screwed them together to form simple structures. He had the following to say on this approach: "A piece of furniture made of high-grade wood and manufactured completely according to traditional production methods is transported in a crate to avoid damage. The recipient at most says: 'well packaged'. However, no one has ever ascertained that such a chest embodies an improvised, highly purposeful method of carpentry. The simple elements of which it is composed make it more stable than its contents. [...] There must therefore at long last be someone who chooses the crate rather than the piece of furniture."
The first series of Rietveld's Krat (= crate) furniture included a chair, a small table and a shelf. These items consisted of simple, standardized boards 14.5 cm and 6.5 cm wide and 45, 60, 70, 90 or 105 cms long, which could be cut to the right length with great ease in

Rietveld's workshop. They were then sold to users as "do-it-yourself" kits and screwed together at home. Anyone who wanted painted furniture, Rietveld recommended, could simply do so prior to assembly so that the screwed, additive construction remained. The way the boards were put together was also devised such that the coarse character of the wood remained visible. Thus, the struts in the Krat chair are positioned along the inner sides of the front legs, but on the outside of the back legs; moreover, the arm-rests appear to lie loose on the vertical legs.

As of 1935, Rietveld drafted further items, such as a chair, a stool, a bed, a shelf and a desk all based on the Krat principle. Metz & Co. now sold them ready assembled and as "week-end furniture".

The fact that the furniture was kept as simple as possible suggests that Rietveld wanted to design objects that were as favorably priced as possible, given the economic problems of the 1930s. Although the Krat furniture was indeed a relative bargain, its unorthodox, farmhouse-like aesthetics encountered much criticism at the time, preventing the furniture from becoming more widespread.

Some of the Krat furniture was produced in the 1970s by Cassina. MK

40

Name: **Scagno**
Designer: **Giuseppe Terragni**
Draft: **approx. 1935/36**
Production: **as of 1972**
Manufacturers: **Zanotta s.p.a.,**
Measurements: **H 80 W 50 D 60, seat height 41 cms**
Materials: **laquered wood, flat steel**

It was not until 1972 that the Scagno chair started to be manufactured, by Zanotta in Italy. Neither original models nor prototypes have survived, nor do we have any indication whether it was ever built during the short life of its creator, Giuseppe Terragni. Although the Terragni Foundation archive possesses only four undated sketches, the chair was probably designed in the mid-1930s (1935/36), approximately contemporaneously with the drafts for the Casa del Fascio residence in Como.

The outstanding feature of the Scagno are the supports made of steel bands and positioned between the square seat and the bent laminated wood back. Their narrow, rectangular cross-section and the fact that a solid raw material is used, necessitate production involving processing unlike that used for the more versatile tubular steel if the result is to exhibit the transparency and elasticity already attained by the innovative drafts of Mart Stam, Marcel Breuer and Mies van der Rohe. Like these designers, Terragni also appears to have striven to

integrate perfectly the formal elements, such as the strictly geometric circular line; in the case of Scagno, the latter serves to emphasize the separation of the individual elements and in this way to distinguish it from the softer and more freely shaped tubular steel furniture of the day. Scagno's almost primitive simplicity brings to mind later, post-modern movements such as the Memphis group, in whose work furniture appears as both sign and means of expression.
It is unclear whether Terragni originally had in mind a chair with one or with two back supports. One of his original sketches shows the chair from the front, with two supports and a molded seat; while another, perspectival sketch presents a version with only one central support and a more abstract, geometrically shaped seat that merges seamlessly with the legs. A further drawing of a side view gives us no indication at to how many back supports were intended. A compromise based on the two variants (with the geometrical seat, but two back supports), the version manufactured today posthumously has contributed decisively to the success of the chair and raised it to the status of a classic. However, it cannot claim without a shadow of doubt to do justice to the designer's actual goals. FZ/MK

41 

Name:	**Siesta Medizinal**
Designers:	**Hans and Wassili Luckhardt**
Draft:	**1936**
Production:	**since 1937**
Manufacturer:	**Gebrüder Thonet AG, Frankenberg on Eder, Germany**
Measurements:	**H 113.5/84; W 67; D 90.5/163; seat height 41 cms**
Materials:	**wood, leather upholstery**

When Le Corbusier, Charlotte Perriand, and Pierre Jeanneret first presented their anatomically shaped, adjustable chaise longue at the end of the twenties, Hans Luckhardt designed, first alone and after 1933/34 together with Anton Lorenz, the so-called "reclining chairs."
At the time, Lorenz concerned himself especially with medical problems associated with sitting. Around 1935 the first trial models were produced by Thonet. On the basis of these trials, Luckhardt developed numerous examples in a line of chaise longues which Thonet marketed as of 1937 under the name Siesta Medizinal. The chair's true innovation lay in the mechanics of its so-called "steering mechanism," which synchronously moved the three separate supports for the back and the upper and lower thighs, ensuring adjustment to each movement of the body automatically by a mere shifting

of weight, and keeping the chair stably balanced at all times. If the user stretches out, the chair stretches with him, extending into a lightly wavy chaise longue or, in the opposite direction, retracting back into a chair position. It can be fixed in any position by a screw attached to the side. The space available is generously proportioned on anatomically shaped slats; armrests and an adjustable headrest round out the comfort of the chair.

Underwater trials, which Lorenz conducted in 1938 at the Kaiser Wilhelm Institute for Industrial Physiology in Dortmund, proved after the fact that the user is in an optimal position for relaxation on the stretched out, slightly wavy surface of the Siesta Medizinal. Luckhardt also created his prototype for the first automatically adjustable airplane seat at the same time as the Siesta Medizinal. It was tested by Air France in 1938 but, due to the outbreak of the war, did not go into mass production. In addition to numerous other versions and further refinements, e.g., as a folding chair, the construction was also marketed by Thonet as a treatment chair made of tubular steel with metal springs for cushioning and armrests which could be adjusted upward. In the fifties, the US patent granted to Anton Lorenz for the mechanism of the chair sparked a huge industry which specialized in the production of reclining chairs. MSC

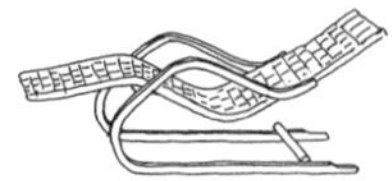

42

Name: **Chaise Longue No. 39**
Designer: **Alvar Aalto**
Draft: **1936**
Production: **1936 to the present**
Manufacturer: **Oy.Huonekalu-ja Rakennustyötehdas AB, Turku, Finland, for Artek Oy. AB, Helsinki**
Measurements: **H 69; W 61; D 161.5 cms**
Materials: **bent, laminated birch wood, tensioned belts**

Chaise Longue No. 39 combines several different aspects in one piece of furniture. It is no doubt a reaction to "Chaise longue à réglage continu," Le Corbusier's tubular steel recliner from 1928. Aaltos chaise longue gives equal consideration to the S-curve, a feature which promotes relaxation, as was confirmed after clinical trials at Dortmund's Kaiser Wilhelm Institute in 1938.

Its cantilevered form, which Aalto had already developed in chairs dating from 1930/31, introduces the spring principle of tubular steel furniture in a wood construction. Although Aalto also designed metal furniture on occasion, he felt that its tactile characteristics and psychological effect were cold and uninviting, while wood struck him as being more pleasant. He was already aware of this in 1929, when he created the furniture for the tuberculosis

sanitarium in Paimio.
Wood was also the material preferred by architects, and it had enjoying a long tradition in rural Finland with its seemingly endless forests. In Finland, weaving textiles and carpets out of paper-twine is one of the oldest crafts. The first versions of the recliner were covered with paper-twine fabric due to the wartime dearth of raw materials. Later versions use fabric covering or leather.
Although the construction of Chaise Longue No. 39 heeds the lessons of previous developmental stages, it takes laminated wood almost to breaking point, since the chair's center of gravity is extremely far away from the leg struts. In other models, Aalto reinforced the points subject to the greatest bending with additional layers of veneer, so that the parts bearing less weight remained slender. However, in the recliner, the supporting elements have the same diameter throughout, and it thus appears more uniform and continuous.
The reclining chair went on public show in 1937 at the world's fair in Paris, in the Finnish pavilion designed by Aalto. The dynamic form of superimposed waves of the armrest and reclining surface anticipates Aalto's "wavy wall" motif, with which he won the competition to design the Finnish pavilion for the New York's world fair in 1939. This motif had an influence on architecture and design until the fifties. PD

43

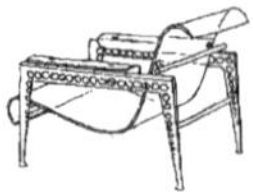

Name:	**(Garden Chair)**
Designer:	**Jacques André**
Draft:	**1936**
Production:	**1937**
Manufacturer:	**Ateliers Jean Prouvé, Nancy**
Measurements:	**H 70; W 74.5; D 97.5; seat height 31,5 cms**
Materials:	**varnished sheet metal, acrylic glass**

Like Jean Prouvé, Jacques André came from a family of architects and craftsmen in Nancy. Their fathers were actively involved in the Ecole de Nancy which played an important role in Art Nouveau. Jean Prouvé was a founding member in 1929 of the avant-garde Union des Artistes Modernes (UAM) and in 1934 recruited Jacques André as well, who had just received his architecture degree and had been working with him since the 1920s.
In 1936 the two of them suggested to UAM on the occasion of the 1937 world's fair in Paris that the union present a comprehensive collection of furniture. The intention was to create a combination of steel with acrylic glass and thus create an equivalent in furniture to high-tech architecture which, through its skeletal steel construction and generous use of glass, created an increasingly light appearance.
Prouvé had produced a prototype for a plexiglass object that same year and had presented it at the Paris autumn salon. In February of 1937, Jacques André began

production of the series which was only intended to comprise six parts. The chair was made of folded and perforated sheet metal and was constructed in Jean Prouvé's workshop. Folding the sheet metal increased its resilience, while perforation reduced the weight and supported the visual sense of dematerialization.
The material acrylic glass only appears to be light and was at that time very difficult to produce and to process. At the presentation of the series in 1937, André also encountered problems with the weatherproofing of the material which tended to develop cracks in direct sunlight. The anticipated positive response was not forthcoming and no producer was found for the production of the series as hoped. MK

44

Name:	**Landi**
Designer:	**Hans Coray**
Draft:	**1938**
Production:	**1939 to the present**
Manufacturer:	**P. & W. Blattmann Metallwarenfabrik, Wädenswil, Switzerland**
Measurements:	**H 77; W 54; D 58; seat height 43 cms**
Materials:	**molded and heat-treated aluminum alloy, stained rubber**

Landi is the official outdoor chair of the Schweizerische Landesausstellung (Swiss National Exhibition), nicknamed the "Landi," which was held in Zurich in 1939.
The "Landi" architect, Hans Fischli, invited submissions to a competition for over 1,500 new chairs for gardens, squares and parks in 1938. Since these were meant to have a link to Switzerland, it was decided that the material of choice be the "Swiss metal," aluminum. Aluminum was one of the most important export articles, stood for modernity, and could only be produced using great quantities of electricity, these being readily available through hydroelectric power plants. As early as November 1933, the parent company of the Schweizerische Aluminiumwerke in Paris had initiated a competition to identify the best aluminum chair. Walter

Gropius and Le Corbusier were members of the jury, and Marcel Breuer won first prize.
1938, Hans Coray, student of Romance languages and self-taught designer, won the first prize of SF 500 with a miniature model consisting of a perforated steel seat with a wire base. The cooperation between Fischli-Coray-Blattmann (the metal-working company) and the Rorschach aluminum works finally resulted in a sensational chair that weighed a mere three kilos. One innovative feature was the development of a shell from a hard material - even prior to the Eameses' attempts at bending metal - which was molded using a 300-ton drawing press. The perforation of the metal, an idea borrowed from the aviation industry, reduced the weight while the three-dimensional shape of the perforation edges improved the stability. The development was supported by concurrent experiments by the Swiss Federal Railway. The base of the feet was also made of molded metal strips, the innovative Argon metal-arc welding joined the identical pairs of legs by the cross beams beneath the seat. All individual parts underwent special heat treatment, rendering the aluminum as hard as steel, and afterward all that remained was to mount the seat on the lower base with screwed connections.
Since the Landi was intended for outdoor use, no caps were placed under the feet. In various stages these were first made of plastic wood, later of plastic, and at the end of the fifties in the present form of black or white rubber since the chair was increasingly used indoors. In 1962 the manufacturers changed the number and arrangement of the perforations, reducing the rows from

7 to 6 and the original 91 holes to 60; after 1971 also marketed under the name 2070 Spartana by Zanotta s.p.a. This enabled mass production rather than individual processing and gave the springy seat greater stability, since in the first models cracks sometimes appeared in the curved area between the seat and the back.
At the end of the "Landi", the chairs were sold to visitors for SF 5. PD

45

Name: **B.K.F., Hardoy Chair**

Designer: **Grupo Austral**
Draft: **1938**
Production: **since 1938**
Manufacturer: **Artek-Pascoe, Inc., New York**
Measurements: **H 93; W 71.5; D 75; seat height 31.5 cms**
Materials: **varnished steel, leather**

This piece of furniture was probably modeled on a folding chair from England patented in 1877. There, four wood crosses connected by joints create a foldable frame over which canvas was stretched for the seat and backrest. Since the chair can be compactly folded and is easy to transport, it was very popular for travel, leisure, and also for homes; and due to its famous owners such as Thomas Alva Edison and Theodore Roosevelt, it soon became famous. From 1905 to the present it has been sold in nearly unchanged form by the American folding and camping furniture producer, Gold Medal, Inc. The Argentineans Bonet, Ferrari-Hardoy, and Kurchan adapted the 1938 design to create a rigid construction made of two loops of bent steel rods welded to each other with leather or fabric covers. In the previous year the three had been apprentices in France with Le Corbusier. It is possible that he became familiar with traditional English folding furniture at that time, for the tubular steel chair Siège à dossier basculant created in

1928 was modeled on a similar chair. With their design, which won a prize in 1940, Ferrari-Hardoy, Kurchan and Bonet succeeded in creating an unusual, timeless piece of furniture: Although the signlike shape has the feel of an abstract improvisation, one reason why the model was very popular in interiors in the fifties, it is simultaneously convincing, given the clear logic of its structure. This bodiless, light chair, which even offers some of the comfort of a club armchair, is one of the most successful seat designs of this century. MSC

Eames
Saarinen
Risom
Thaden
Prouvé

5

1941-1950

Design during World War II

World War II brought artistic and cultural life to a complete standstill throughout Europe. Artists, designers and architects, in so far as they were not driven into exile, had neither the financial resources nor the necessary materials to realize their ideas.

While civil sciences and research stagnated, all resources were committed to the production of **war materials**. Thus, airplane technology makes a leap forward with the development of **jets**. Major advances are also made in the **plastics industry**, which, since the 1930s, had been a branch of industry undergoing steady growth.

In the USA, away from the arena of war, somewhat better working conditions existed for designers. Given the large public interest in organic and streamlined design, a very promising alternative to the strictly rectangular drafts of the European avant-garde, the New York **Museum of Modern Art** (MoMA) launched, in 1940, its competition for "**Organic Design in Home Furnishings**". **Charles Eames** (46, 48, 50, 52, 64, 67) and **Eero Saarinen** (46, 65) won the competition with designs for chairs which, for the first time, make use of seats produced using three-dimensional molded wood laminates.

The MoMA organized a further competition in 1948 entitled **"Low-Cost Furniture Design"**. Given the dire economic straits and lack of resources at the end of the war, the competition was intended to attract furniture designs which took these new conditions into account.

Among other things, one of the first chairs featuring a **seat made of plastic** was entered in the competition, again a design by Charles Eames. This time he utilized knowledge gained in producing plastic sheaths for radar antennae in World War II.

It was not until the end of the 1940s that the economic situation in Europe had improved sufficiently to afford designers a renewed favorable domain for their ideas. However, the price of a product became an even more important criterion than before the War.

The beginning of the **Cold War** led, in the Communist world, to an age in which design as a free creative process, played a subordinate role.

46

Name:	**Organic Armchair**
Designers:	**Charles Eames and Eero Saarinen**
Draft:	**1940**
Production:	**1941**
Manufacturers:	**Haskelite Corporation, Chicago, Illinois together with Heywood-Wakefield Company,Gardner, Massachusetts, and Marli Ehrman**
Measurements:	**H 92.5; W 75; D 62.5; seat height 40 cms**
Materials:	**molded plywood, birch wood, foam rubber, fabric**

On October 1, 1940, the Department of Industrial Design at the Museum of Modern Art in New York announced a nationwide design competition, with the goal of enhancing the level of private interiors of all classes of society through a cooperative effort between designers, manufacturers, and dealers. The theme of the competition was "Organic Design in Home Furnishings," with organic design defined as follows: "A design can be called organic if, within the object as a whole, there is a harmonious relationship between the individual elements as regards structure, material, and purpose." The competition was supported by twelve renowned American department stores, who promised to sign contracts with manufacturers; one of the conditions of the competition was that the design be feasible on an industrial scale.

The jury members included, among others, Marcel Breuer and Alvar Aalto, whose chair made of two-dimensionally formed plywood was exhibited at the MoMA in 1938. Charles Eames and Eero Saarinen won two first prizes within the six furniture categories. Especially noteworthy were chair and armchair designs in the category entitled "Seating for a Living Room."

Starting in July 1941, Charles and Ray Eames began developing a process for the three-dimensional molding of plywood in their Los Angeles apartment with the intention of producing first-class models with it. They fashioned a plaster inverse chair shell, which could be heated with electric heating elements. They covered this shell with several layers of veneer, the fibers running in alternating directions, and between each of these they placed a foil made of hot-melt adhesive. After sealing the mold, which they called the "Kazam!machine" owing to the noise it made, a bicycle pump was used to press a membrane against the veneer layers so that these clung to the inverse shell and melted the adhesive. Within four to six hours, the pressing procedure was finished. By making incisions in and cutting out pieces of the veneer, a three-dimensional form emerged.

In keeping with the competition guidelines, Haskelite was entrusted with producing the shell, while Heywood-Wakefield was in charge of lining it with a thin layer of foam rubber. Fabric designer and Bauhaus student Marli Ehrman created the cover.
In the intervening time before the inauguration of the exhibition in September 1941 at the MoMA, several chairs and armchairs were produced. The legs were made of solid birch wood instead of aluminum as intended, for the latter was not available due to the war. The backs of the chairs were not, as originally planned, a bare wood shell, since at this stage the veneer was invariably susceptible to damage.
Because of the war, and the fact that production costs were still high, the prototype did not go into serial production, thus missing the original point of the competition. PD

47

Name:	**Chair No. 654 W**
Designer:	**Jens Risom**
Draft:	**1941/42**
Production:	**approx. 1942-1955**
Manufacturer:	**Hans Knoll Furniture, New York**
Measurements:	**H 75.5; W 52; D 72 cms**
Materials:	**laminated wood, nylon covering**

Jens Risom studied interior and furniture design under Kaare Klint at the College of Arts and Crafts in Copenhagen.

In 1939, he emigrated to the US, where he initially made his living as a textile designer. That same year, however, Risom was able to realize his first furniture designs through his work with Hans Knoll, a young furniture dealer who had immigrated from Germany. Knoll's stand at the 1939 World Fair in New York featured two interiors designed by Risom. In the first Hans G. Knoll Furniture catalog, which came out in 1942, 15 of the 25 models offered were Risom's work, including a series of chairs made of laminated wood and spanned with fabric belts, which met with considerable success.

In terms of outward appearance, these chairs remained true to the tradition of solid, restrained modernity which Scandinavian design had already popularized during the 1930s. The organic designs by Finnish designer Alvaar Aalto were characterized by the absence of right angles, for example, and Risom took the idea of covering the chair with belts from Bruno Matthson, who had been employing this form of upholstery since 1936. The most remarkable design in the Knoll series, shown here, is a low, curved armchair with boomerang-shaped side elements. It calls to mind similar designs by Matthson dating back to 1934, yet also reveals the influence of the aesthetics of streamlining which emerged in nearly all design fields at this time in the US.

It was no easy task to have furniture serially produced during World War II, for the scarcity of resources forced the American government to prohibit or limit the use of certain materials. Thus, during the war the Knoll company had to cover the chairs with nylon from discarded army equipment. The simple, standardized frame components, originally made of cedarwood, enabled the chair to be assembled quickly and cheaply. After the war, hardwood became available once again, and laminated beechwood was used for the frames.

In 1948, Hans Knoll sold the license to produce the chairs to the furniture company owned by his father, Walter Knoll, in Germany. There, marketed as "Vostra", it became just as popular as it had been in the United States. In the years that followed, Scandinavian designs became the quintessence of a modern European style that found its way into numerous homes owing to its use of natural materials and straightforward formal idiom. MK

48

Name: LCW (Lounge Chair Wood)
Designers: Charles and Ray Eames
Draft: 1945
Production: 1946-1957
Manufacturer: Molded Plywood Division of the Evans Products Company, Venice, CA, for Herman Miller Furniture Company, Zeeland, Michigan
Measurements: H 68; W 56; D 62; seat height 39 cms
Materials: molded plywood, rubber

Following the MoMA's "Organic Design in Home Furnishings" exhibition, Charles and Ray Eames continued to advance the three-dimensional molding of plywood. In December 1941, an acquaintance of theirs, Dr. Wendel G. Scott, called to their attention the fact that the Navy had no suitable leg splints for injured soldiers. In just over a year, Charles and Ray Eames were able to produce appropriate prototypes, and in November 1942 received the Navy's first order for 5,000 molded plywood leg splints. Together with former colleagues, they a set up a production company and research lab, the Plyformed Wood Company. Further commissions followed from the army, and Charles Eames became head of research in

the Molded Plywood Division at the Evans Product Company, which, among other things, developed molded plywood parts for airplanes. He and his staff acquired valuable technological experience which proved useful when they began concentrating on civil projects after the war was over.
Their interest continued to focus on the development and production of inexpensive, fashionable furniture while taking into account the general scarcity of raw materials. The plywood technology met two criteria: it ensured frugal use of materials and offered comfort, for the furniture was molded to the human body.
The DCW (Dining Chair Wood) and the LCW were the first items to enjoy high popularity. The Organic Armchair, from 1940/41, had already revealed the difficulties involved in forming a complete chair shell with complex curve radii from plywood. The Eameses treated the different functions of the shell independently, so that the convex forms did not have to be as strong. Furthermore, the modular character of the design yielded a number of possible combinations of the seat and backrest, with various foot rests available either in laminated wood or metal. These were initially attached with elastic rubber shock mounts that were firmly welded to the wood using a modified Chrysler process.
In the autumn of 1945, Molded Plywood Division produced a number of chairs and armchairs from a wide variety of woods, with fabric, imitation leather, leather, or hide coverings for the seat and backrest; Evans Products organized marketing and distribution.

The prototypes were presented to the press in December 1945 at a preview showing at the Barclay Hotel in New York. In February 1946 they were displayed at an Architectural League exhibition and finally, in March 1946, in a solo MoMA exhibition entitled "New Furniture - Designed by Charles Eames" in New York.

While Evans Products delayed expanding its furniture branch, the new design director at the Herman Miller Furniture Company, George Nelson, came across the plywood furniture as a result of these publicity activities. The companies worked out a cooperation agreement in which the Molded Plywood Division guaranteed production and Herman Miller took over marketing. Serial production began in mid-1946. The unusually high degree of publicity which Herman Miller Furniture achieved with the Eames Plywood Collection induced the company to acquire the production rights in 1949. At that point, Charles Eames had already been working as a design consultant for Herman Miller for two years. PD

49

Name:	**(Plywood Chair)**
Designer:	**H. V. Thaden**
Draft:	**1947**
Production:	**unknown**
Manufacturer:	**Thaden Jordan Furniture Corporation, Roanoke, Virginia**
Measurements:	**H 109/98; W 50; D 69/84; seat height 29/22,5 cms**
Materials:	**bent plywood, metal, wood**

This chair was presumably intended as an experiment and was never produced in a larger series. The back and seat consist of a single bent plywood panel, the front edge covered with a protective rod to prevent the edge from being broken. A second plywood panel, its edge similarly protected, serves as a rear support that can be locked in at two different heights. It is reinforced by a third, thinner piece of plywood, which is braced between the seat and the rod in back.

As early as 1874, Isaac Cole registered a patent on a chair made of bent plywood with a shape nearly identical to the one shown here. It was followed by similar designs by August Thonet around 1900 and by Alvar Aalto in the thirties.

Because the material is not particularly strong, it is doubtful whether Thaden's construction could have withstood normal use. However, it was certainly more than mere aesthetic considerations that led to this spectacular design. The construction is extremely clever, even if it is not practicable in this form. Particularly original is the use of slot-in connectors for the height-adjustable joint between the backrest and the supports. In those days, this kind of fastener was found primarily in airplanes, boats, or automobiles, where it was used to secure tarpaulins or convertible tops. During the forties, aviation was the source of many innovations in furniture design. The shape of the chair, which seems to hover in the air much like an airplane wing, suggests that it may indeed have derived its inspiration from this source. MSC

50

Name:	**RAR (Rocking Armchair with Rod-Base)**
Designer:	**Charles and Ray Eames/University of California, Los Angeles**
Design:	**1948**
Production:	**1950-1968**
Manufacturer:	**Zenith Plastics, Gardena, California, for Herman Miller Furniture Company, Zeeland, Michigan**
Measurements:	**Size: 75 x 63 x 62; seat height 43 cms**
Materials:	**fiberglass, round steel bars, wood**

The "RAR" armchair was designed in 1948. It belongs to a group of shell chairs and armchairs with a variety of bases which Charles and Ray Eames entered for the international competition for "Low-Cost Furniture Design" at the New York MoMA. Although the Eameses also submitted a design for a chair made of fiberglass-reinforced plastic (see "La Chaise"), the actual intention was to make the chairs using varnished or Neoprene-coated steel or sheet aluminum. The couple worked closely with engineers at the University of California in Los Angeles, producing several aluminum prototypes, a task that

proved to be unusually difficult because the provisional molded forms kept bursting.
In the eyes of the jury, which included Ludwig Mies van der Rohe, making seating furniture out of sheet metal held promise as a method of mass production, and had even proven useful in the automobile industry. Thus, the first prize went to a sheet metal chair by Don R. Knorr, and the shell chair series by Charles and Ray Eames placed second. While drawings and plaster models were acceptable for the competition, the planned exhibition of the prize-winning pieces was to show realistic prototypes for mass production. As a result, the exhibition date was continually put back, until the show finally opened in March 1950. Meanwhile, Irv Green, Sol Fingerhut and Milt Brucker of Zenith Plastics presented their fiberglass process at the Eameses' studio. This technology had been developed during the war for radar housing (Radom) on the noses of airplanes. In cooperation with the Herman Miller Furniture Company, the first series of 2,000 armchair shells was manufactured by hand - still with a cord embedded around the edge for reinforcement - and displayed at the Chicago Showroom and the Museum of Modern Art in New York.
With a patent for welded-on shock mounts developed by Chrysler, it was possible to mount the shell-shaped seats dyed in different colors on different bases without having to alter the shell. This enabled the hydraulically controlled positive/negative metal molds to be produced efficiently while retaining the greatest

variation among the models. With the series of shell chairs and armchairs, the formal ideas central to the Organic Armchair designed by Charles Eames and Eero Saarinen in 1940 (see above) were brought to bear in mass production via a detour into concepts for metal furniture that was never manufactured.
Up until 1968 the RAR was produced by Herman Miller as a luxury model of this series, and even as late as 1984 employees were presented with a copy of RAR on the birth of a child. PD

51

Name: Antony (Chair for the student dormitory in Antony)
Designer: Jean Prouvé
Draft: 1950
Production: approx. 1950-55
Manufacturer: Studio Jean Prouvé, Nancy
Measurements: H 86.5, W 50.5, D 68 cms
Materials: bent plywood, lacquered steel tubing, lacquered steel sheet

Jean Prouvé, architect, engineer and designer, endeavored by using highly-developed technologies for metal processing to achieve innovative constructions and forms in his design and architecture work. He played a decisive part in developing construction techniques using leight-weight prefabricated parts in architecture, making use, among other things, of insights from the airplane and automotive industry. In his Atelier Jean Prouvé, the company he founded in 1947, he started not only producing light-weight components but also his own design drafts.
In 1955, Prouvé participated, together with the French designer group Union des Artistes Modernes (which supported its members in participating in public tenders), in the competition for furnishings for the student dormitory in Antony, near Paris. Co-operating with Charlotte Perriand, he manufactured an exemplary

furniture series for the common rooms, the cafeterias and a series of rooms in the dormitory. They included the chair shown here, which Prouvé had drafted as early as 1950 for the University of Strasbourg.
In contrast to the technical appearance of Prouvé's early drafts, the aesthetic subtlety of this furniture already reveals influences from art of the post-war era, which emphasized free and organic forms. The curved seat seems to be weightless, since it is joined only at four points to the base. Steel bearing elements and tubular steel legs are a variation on a similar form and juxtaposed to each other as contrasts.
Nevertheless, Prouvé's technical approach remains evident. He chose tubular steel for the legs of the chair for reasons of costs, the bearing elements are made of solid steel, which can likewise be cut simply and advantageously. The central axle made of a single thick steel tube enables the legs to be connected simply and stably with the bearing elements. At the same time this axis suggests a swivel mechanism, which, like the parabolic form of the bearing elements, is reminiscent of the machine-like functions of earlier Prouvé designs. MK

If we could read the design through the toy filter, perhaps we could produce a special hope: it is a way to go back to innocence.

Ettore Sottsass, Designer, 1997

6

Eames
Bloc
Mategot
Ponti
Bertoia
Perriand
Yanagi
Guhl
Castiglioni
Jacobsen
Nelson
Saarinen
Panton
Zanuso
Sapper

1951-1960

Mass Products for the Economic Miracle

In Europe, the post-War years were characterized by a prevailing longing for security and an orderly life. Not least owing to the financial and material aid received from the US, the economies in the war-torn countries rapidly improved. The United States also set the standards in Europe with regard to what was held to be progress and fashion. **Cars, refrigerators, televisions, washing machines** or **record players** become generally affordable and invade the household and leisure time. The results of the war effort in the **plastics sector** are now applied to civilian purposes and processes, spawning everyday objects such as **nylons, Tupperware** or **plastic seating**. Plastics such as polyesters or polyamide are easy to dye, weigh little, can replace or imitate other materials and are thus ideally suitable for the industrial production of bargain-basement consumer goods. **Fashion cycles** change ever more rapidly, and the design of **non-reusable products** together inaugurate the triumphal procession of plastics and create new challenges for the designers to face.
In Italy, in 1957 the first professional association for industrial design was founded, the Associazione per il Disegno Industriale (**ADI**). Pioneers such as **Achille Castiglioni** (60, 79)**, Marco Zanuso** (68)**, Ettore Sottsass** (89) or **Giò Ponti** (55) create a strong basis for the international reputation of Italian design; it is soon regarded as the epitome of a creative, imaginative

approach to problems of product design.
In addition to Italian drafts, Scandinavian design was also catching the attention. With plain and high-grade furniture, designers such as **Arne Jacobsen** (61) or **Hans Wegner** (72) found a new interpretation for the long Scandinavian tradition of wood processing and set themselves off with this bridge between Modernism and the 1950s from the numerous short-lived and eclectic drafts of the day.
In Germany, a movement developed out of the Ulm **College of Design** founded in 1955, which, as the **"Ulm school"**, took up the strictly rationalist approach of the Bauhaus. In co-operation with the **Braun** company, representatives of the movements also developed the concept of a so-called **corporate identity** - intended not only to cover the full range of products, but all areas of a company, in other words all print matter, display rooms or advertising campaigns.
Innovative, North American furniture design was shaped by fruitful competition between the Hermann Miller and Knoll firms. While Hermann Miller worked together with **Charles Eames** (46, 48, 50, 52, 54, 67) and **George Nelson** (62, 63), among other things Knoll brought out designs by **Eero Saarinen** (64, 65) and **Harry Bertoia** (56). Almost simultaneously, Eames and Bertoia create the first chairs using seats made of wire mesh.
The sub-division of the chair into an ergonomic seat and base that often appeared fragile is a feature developed, above all, by Eames in many of his drafts of the 1950s. These collage-like combinations of contrasting elements allude to the art of the day, in which **Joan Miró,**

Alexander Calder or **Jean Arp** are representative of comparable trends.

52

Name: **DKR (Dining Height, K-Wire Shell, R-Wire Base/Rod Iron Base)**
Designers: **Charles and Ray Eames**
Draft: **1951**
Production: **1951-1967**
Manufacturer: **Banner Metals, Compton, California, for Herman Miller Furniture Company, Zeeland, Michigan**
Measurements: **H 82; W 48; D 52.5; seat height 45.5 cms**
Materials: **varnished wire**

Charles and Ray Eames demonstrated their fondness for industrial production methods and materials with a technological thrust in their designs for the New York MoMA's 1948 "Low-Cost Furniture Design" competition. After rejecting the idea of an organic, i.e. human-body-shaped, shell designed of pressed sheet steel or aluminum, and modifying the use of fiberglass technology, Charles and Ray Eames duplicated the shape of the S-Shell (Side-Chair) using welded wire. The choice of wire was certainly influenced by Harry Bertoia who, as a sculptor, employed metal wire and pipes and had worked in the Eameses' office from 1943 to 1946. In 1952, just one year following the marketing introduction of the DKR, Bertoia introduced his Diamond Chair to the public which was produced by Knoll. In a lawsuit between Herman Miller and Knoll, Charles and Ray Eames were awarded intellectual ownership of the copyright. Wire had already proven itself as a material in various bases for fiberglass shells and for the bases of tables. Its delicate transparency and visual lightness combined with high resiliency could now also be applied to the shell construction. After experiments with triangular mesh, a rectangular structure and spot-welding were eventually chosen. The loose ends of wire were bound at the edge by two thicker wires. Thus the tips of the wires were less sharp and the shell shape was stabilized. This technological innovation was awarded a patent, the first for a mechanical solution for furniture. With its use of a single material for the base and seat the design of the Wire Chair, as the DKR is also known, offered a holistic appearance, but, like the plastic shell, it was also available in different base options; the most well known is the "Eiffel-Tower Base."

It proved possible to enhance seating comfort on the rigid wire chair additionally by a single - or, after 1955, a two-piece (bikini version) - removable, thin cushion. This allowed a variety of possibilities for combining individual parts and different colors. In 1952, the Wire Chair was awarded the Trail Blazer Award by the Home Fashions League of America. The Wire Chair has been manufactured and marketed by Vitra AG, Basel since 1958. PD

53

Name:	**Bellevue (Chair for the Bellevue House)**
Designer:	**André Bloc**
Draft:	**1951**
Production:	**unknown**
Manufacturer:	**André Bloc, Meudon**
Measurements:	**H 82.5; W 39.5; D 49; seat height 42 cms**
Materials:	**bent plywood, varnished steel**

Furniture designs by architect André Bloc were greatly influenced by the works of sculptor Jean Arp. Arp's flowing forms, which are often abstractions of the human body, served as Bloc's inspiration for this design as well.
There are only a few copies of the chair, which was most likely produced expressly for his Bellevue house in Meudon. Some of them feature a V-shaped metal frame which makes up the rear legs, while others are supported at the back by two separate metal legs. All models have a backrest and seat made of a single piece of material - an S-shaped curve.
Attempts to create the front legs, back and seat of a chair using just one piece of bent wood had already met with success. The first was Isaac Cole in 1880, and then, at the turn of the century, August Thonet. To create a visual unity, Cole and Thonet glued the separate back support to the backrest to engender

one single form. Rietveld's Zig-Zag chair combined a wood back, seat, and frame into a unit that was visually excellent, but a failure as a structure. Bloc, on the other hand, believed that function transformed into pure form would no longer possess any superfluous features. As he could not make all of his chair parts from one casting, he let the contrasts remain and instead minimized the difficulties involved in the construction.

A desk designed by André Bloc at around the same time similarly involves a simple, sculptural construction. PR

54

Name:	**Chaise Nagasaki**
Designer:	**Mathieu Matégot**
Draft:	**1952**
Production:	**1952-1959**
Manufacturers:	**Société Matégot, Paris**
Measurements:	**H 74; W 56.5; D 58 cms**
Materials:	**tubular steel, perforated varnished sheet metal**

After studying at the Academy of Art in Budapest, Mathieu Matégot returned to France in 1939 to volunteer as a soldier. When the war was over, he worked in France as a textile designer and achieved international acclaim with his rug designs. Matégot also founded a furniture design studio in 1945, which soon employed a staff of 20 and produced furniture and accessories in small series.

As a furniture designer, Matégot's claim to fame was the fact that he was among the first to use perforated sheet metal in his designs. He had hit upon the idea while he was a prisoner of war in Germany, where he used it to build a hand cart, and in 1945, he returned to the idea of incorporating this industrial semi-finished product in his work. It was excellently suited to the work methods employed in Matégot's studio, for it was possible to shape it as desired simply by cutting and bending, and was furthermore inexpensive and extremely light-weight. Matégot used it in combination with tubular steel, bent iron, rattan, wood and plastic.

In 1952, he designed the Nagasaki chair, one of his best known and most successful models. Two bent tubular steel elements are welded together to support the seat shell and the backrest. The transparency of the two shells accents the minimalist construction and the refracted light lends the surface a shimmering moirée effect. Matégot highlighted the collage-like composition of the individual elements by painting the seat red or yellow, thus setting it off from the rest of the chair.

The Nagasaki chair evidences a clear, visible separation of the constructive elements into seat shell and frame - a typical design feature of the 1950s. Designers such as Charles Eames made use of this distinction in an attempt to optimize the technology of the individual functions and the overall structure of the chairs. Matégot, however, never regarded himself as an industrial designer, and preferred to compare his workshop to the ateliers of Parisian couturiers. He focused specifically on simple craftsmanship and the aesthetics of the chair, preserving the nearly raw character of the original industrial materials to create chairs that even today seem futuristic. MK

55 

Name:	**No. 699, Superleggera**
Designer:	**Gio Ponti**
Draft:	**1951-1957**
Production:	**1957 to the present**
Manufacturer:	**Figli di Amedeo Cassina, Meda, Milan**
Measurements:	**H 82.5; W 40; D 44.5; seat height 45.5 cms**
Materials:	**varnished ash wood, Spanish cane**

Ponti himself describes this chair as the "normal," "true" chair, the "chair-chair devoid of adjectives." With it, the architect pursued his own standard of keeping things to a bare minimum. At the same time, Ponti's interest in classic forms finds expression in the chair, just as it does in his buildings. Ponti borrowed the concept for Superleggera (super-lightweight) from a series of simple, traditional chairs that have been produced since the nineteenth century in a plant near the Ligurian fishing village of Chiavari. Their stable, lightweight construction and low price made them extremely popular. Ponti was inspired to optimize the qualities of this model during the postwar era, when furnishings were out of necessity frugal.

In his first drafts from 1949, he altered the basic form of the Chiavari chair with an ergonomic bend in the backrest and tapered the legs toward the bottom. He then designed the Leggera for Cassina in 1951, which reduced the structure of the Chiavari chair to only what was absolutely necessary. It was very similar to the Superleggera, but with rods for legs and struts in the backrest. Although the model met with great success among consumers, Ponti strove for even greater perfection and designed the Superleggera for Cassina in 1957, using light, stable ash wood and a seat that was either upholstered or covered with a weave of cane or colored cellophane. Ponti reduced the round cuts of wood to a triangular cross section with edges only 18 mm long, and devised an ingenious system of slot-in connectors in which the individual struts are inserted firmly inside one another: the result is a stable chair weighing a mere 1.7 kilo. To put these to the test, Ponti threw the chair from the fourth story of an apartment building into the street, where it bounced like a ball without breaking. MSC

56

Name: No. 422, Diamond Chair
Designer: Harry Bertoia
Draft: 1952/53
Production: 1953 to the present
Manufacturer: Knoll Associates, Inc., New York
Measurements: H 71; W 110.5; D 81; seat height 36.5 cms
Materials: varnished steel wire, round iron, rubber

Harry Bertoia, who came from Italy, originally dedicated himself to sculpting. While heading the metal workshop of the Cranbrook Academy in Michigan from 1939-1943, he began to experiment with flowing, three-dimensional shapes. At Cranbrook he became acquainted with Eliel and Eero Saarinen as well as Charles Eames and his later wife, Ray Kaiser, as well as Florence Schuster, later wife of the furniture producer Knoll. In 1943 Charles and Ray Eames persuaded Bertoia to move to California, where he cooperated on the development of their first pieces of furniture. Disappointed that his contribution to these joint designs was not recognized, he left the studio in 1946. Hans Knoll, director of the company, whose program already included the designs of well-known architects and designers, equipped him with a studio of his own in 1950 as well as a monthly allowance and the possibility of freely developing his creativity without any special constraints. Bertoia thereupon created a series of chairs and seats using techniques he was familiar with from gold work and sculpting with iron wire. Until 1953 he developed these ideas together with specialists from the Knoll company until they were ready for mass production. At the same time, the first wire chairs were created by Charles and Ray Eames but were presented nearly a year earlier. Bertoia's series consists of a small and large version of the Diamond Chair, a Diamond Chair with an extended back, a foot stool, a children's chair, two other chairs, and a bar stool. Knoll marketed these pieces, which were suited for indoor and outdoor use, first in painted black metal and later with a black or white plastic coating, as well as in chrome and with removable pads. The structure of the Diamond Chair clearly separates the different functions of the chair: the transparent wire shell is bent out of a quadratic lattice into an organically shaped diamond like a net frozen in space, and the base of round iron embraces it like a polished diamond. Bertoia considered his furniture to resemble his sculptures and explained: "In sculpture I am primarily interested in the relationship between form and space and the characteristics of the metal. In chairs many functional problems have to be solved first ... but basically chairs are also studies in space, form and metal. On close inspection it becomes clear that they are mostly made up of air.... Space flows right through them." The generous dimensions of the Diamond Chair, with its projecting armrests and hard rubber connections that noticeably give way with pressure, definitely lent an element of comfort to the mathematical coolness of the construction. But the cushioning still does not make any formal sense despite the comfort it affords, since it interferes with the transparency of the chair and gives it the look of a common shell. The Diamond Chair was designed to be viewed from all sides like a sculpture and thus fits perfectly into the elegant, sparsely furnished interiors of the fifties. The chair was, however, quite expensive even though Bertoia had developed a machine for bending the wires three-dimensionally; production was difficult because the preshaped wires had to be individually welded together. The susceptible rubber pieces were later replaced by screwed metal tracks. Bertoia wrote: "I was never satisfied with my own designs, no matter whether they were flops or masterpieces," and, after completing his line of furniture for Knoll, dedicated himself exclusively to art, including numerous large-scale sculptures which graced the buildings of famous architects. MSC

57

Name:	**Ombre**
Designer:	**Charlotte Perriand**
Draft:	**1953-1955**
Production:	**1955**
Manufacturers:	**Takashimaya, Tokyo**
Measurements:	**H 67; W 44; D 52 cms; seat height 41 cms**
Materials:	**laminated wood, varnished black**

Charlotte Perriand was one of the first great female furniture designers. After studying to become an interior designer, she worked from 1929 until 1937 in the studio of architect Le Corbusier. In 1940, she was hired by the Japanese government as an industrial design consultant to support the local industry there, with the task of developing export goods on the basis of traditional crafts. In 1943, at the end of her time in this position, she organized an exhibition in co-operation with the Takashimaya department store in Tokyo and Osaka. Entitled "Tradition, Selection, Création", it presented model products which were the result of her work in Japan. After a lengthier stay working in what was then Indochina, Perriand returned to France, where she worked as an interior designer and industrial designer.
In 1955, she organized another exhibition at Takashimaya, called "Synthèse des Arts", where modern European interior design was represented by Perriand's furniture, ceramics by Fernand Léger and tapestries by Le

Corbusier. Charlotte Perriand designed shelves, a table, a double recliner and chairs specially for this exhibition. The metal elements for this furniture were produced in the factory owned by architect Jean Prouvé in Nancy, with whom Perriand collaborated on numerous projects. All the wooden parts, on the other hand, were made in Japan. The inter-cultural dialogue inspired by this exhibition continued when, in 1957, Perriand organized an exhibition in Paris that focused on traditional Japanese interior culture.

The black stackable chairs that were grouped around a large dining table at "Synthèse des Arts" clearly show the degree to which Charlotte Perriand was influenced by Japan. While the rich black varnish and the balanced lines lend the chairs the strength and impressiveness of Japanese Kanji characters, the careful application of black varnish to the surface calls to mind the Japanese woodworking tradition, in which varnish plays an important role. The fact that the chairs are stackable reflects the Far Eastern preference for space-saving, mobile furnishings.

By contrast, the construction is typically European in that it consists of just one piece of material, a concept which many avant-garde designers have worked with since the 1920s. Perriand had the front legs, rear legs and back-rest from a single sheet of laminated wood, and then bent the pieces into the desired shape. To avoid having to mold the wood using a laborious three-dimensional bending process, she divided the back-rest into two pieces, each of which was then bent slightly backwards on the inside. In doing so, she achieved a comfortable form that takes into account the shape of the body, and at the same time increased the flexibility of the back-rest. This molding process saved on material, and was no doubt part of the know-how that Charlotte Perriand brought to Japan in her capacity as a consultant. However, her chair design showed that non-European inspirations can help European designers create original, exciting works. Following the "Synthèse des Arts" exhibition, the chair was produced on a small scale and sold by Galerie Steph Simon in Paris. MK

58

Name:	**Butterfly**
Designer:	**Sori Yanagi**
Draft:	**1954**
Production:	**since 1954**
Manufacturer:	**Tendo Mokko Co., Ltd., Tokyo**
Measurements:	**H 41.5; W 47.5; D 34; seat height 35 cms**
Materials:	**bent plywood, brass**

The postwar years in Japan were marked by the reconstruction effort. As Japan was under the supreme command of the Allied Forces, the Institute of Industrial Art was instructed to develop furniture and electrical appliances for houses for the occupation forces and to produce them throughout the entire country as quickly as possible. The scheme lasted until 1947, and, based on American models, led the Japanese to adopt Western technology. Americanisms permeated daily Japanese life; and the influence of Western style remains undiminished even today. In 1950, when the Korean War broke out, Japan profited immensely as a neighboring country and experienced a tremendous economic upswing.
This upswing was fueled further when the occupation of Japan ended in 1951. Renewed independence led to the founding of numerous companies, universities, and cultural establishments. In 1952 Sori Yanagi was among the founders of the Industrial Design

Association (JIDA) and the Japan Design Committee, which had set itself the task of fostering the influence of designers within company hierarchies, for they had previously been excluded from decision-making processes: their job consisted solely in lending existing products a new (in other words, Western) look. That same year, Yanagi opened his own design studio and won first prize for a turntable in the very first Japanese design competition.

Against this background, the Butterfly stool can be regarded as extraordinary for several reasons. Yanagi borrows no known Western forms. This is all the more astonishing given that he spent a great deal of time with Charlotte Perriand between 1940-2, and later as well. She went to Japan on the invitation of the Japanese Secretary of Commerce and Industry to give design a new orientation. Yanagi was at that time a French student, and accompanied Charlotte Perriand on her travels through Japan, thus becoming acquainted with the European classic Modernity. This was quite possibly the source of Yanagi's interest in seating furniture, which did not exist in Japanese culture. Even today many urban households are quite content without any seating furniture whatsoever; traditionally, one sits on tatami mats on the floor.

Yanagi used the plywood molding technique made famous by the Eameses to mass-produce the stool at the Tendo Mokko Company. The stool features an unusually clever construction: two identical forms are attached together symmetrically around the axis using two screws underneath the seat and a threaded brass rod. This yields a shape which on the one hand is reminiscent of the torii (portals) of Shinto shrines and is thus Asian in expression; on the other hand, it resembles the wings of a butterfly, from which it derives its name. In 1957 the stool was awarded a gold medal at the Milan Triennial. PD

59

Name:	**(Garden Chair)**
Designer:	**Willy Guhl**
Draft:	**1954**
Production:	**1954-1980**
Manufacturer:	**Eternit AG, Niederurnen, Switzerland**
Measurements:	**H 54,5; W 54,5;D 76.5 cms; seat height 11 cms**
Materials:	**fibrated concrete**

Willy Guhl was a pioneer of industrial design in Switzerland, both as a result of teaching for many years at the Technical College in Zurich and through his many-sided practical work. He created a number of designs for Eternit: window boxes, a spindle-shaped standing ashtray, and a beach and garden chair, which is unique in the history of furniture design.
After participating in the 1948 MoMA competition entitled "Low-Cost Furniture Design", he began working with casts of the human body and ergonomically shaped shells for reclining chairs. While previous work with laminated wood had already yielded two-dimensionally shaped chairs shells, fibrated concrete - not a material typically associated with furniture-making - afforded new possibilities that Willy Guhl turned to his best advantage.
Fibrated concrete was manufactured in slabs with

machines and was used for building houses. The method of processing the chair corresponds to the dimensions of these slabs, which were shaped directly after they had been pressed while still moist. Thus, production was inexpensive and required fewer materials.

Because the composite material offered great resistance to breakage and exceptional tensile strength, supporting structures were no longer required, and thanks to statics there were few limitations on the form. So the design could be minimalist, rendering the elegantly curved, absolutely weatherproof chair nearly an abstract sculpture.

The new leisure culture of the postwar era gave rise to the need for inexpensive, practical outdoor seating. At the same time, the chair is suggestive of interiors of the sixties and seventies, with their similar curved forms.

Fibrated cement has not been used since the end of the seventies, when it was discovered that the asbestos it contains is a carcinogen. Willy Guhl's chair was also affected by this discovery: one of the last known copies was to be included in the MoMA design collection, but was promptly sent back following the discovery that the chair contained asbestos. The Vitra Design Museum has sealed the surface of its copy so that a piece of design history may be preserved. MK

60

Name:	**Mezzadro**
Designers:	**Achille and Pier Giacomo Castiglioni**
Draft:	**1954-1957**
Production:	**1970 to the present**
Manufacturer:	**Zanotta s.p.a., Nova Milanese, Milan**
Measurements:	**H 52; W 49; D 53,5; seat height 52 cms**
Materials:	**chromed steel, beech wood, lacquered sheet steel**

The first model of the Mezzadro (sharecropper) was presented at the X. Milan Triennial in 1954. It was part of the theme "Art and Production," and belonged conceptually to the section of industrial design which was mainly devised by the Castiglioni brothers. Within the scope of the exhibition, they presented around 150 design objects from all over the world, organizing these according to formal and typological aspects. Drawings, photos and especially informative semifinished products were displayed as explanations for the objects. At the dawn of the era of the rejuvenation of the Italian economy, people in Italy were not merely concerned with satisfying primary functional needs but in infusing everyday culture with some kind of aesthetics. Thus, it was not enough for form to follow function - the main tenet of

Functionalism. Instead, the functions were analyzed so as to determine their optimal visual form. In order to do this, Achille and Pier Giacomo Castiglioni drew on well-known forms which they felt left no room for improvement, and related them to one another in new contexts. This procedure for objets trouvés or ready-mades brings to mind works by Marcel Duchamp or, to a limited extent, those of Pablo Picasso.

The Castiglionis used a typical tractor seat for their springy metal seat, and attached it with a bicycle wing nut to a swinging strip steel bow, which in a tractor absorbs the jolts that result from driving on uneven ground. They stabilized the reduced cantilever-base chair (see Mies van der Rohe's preference for strip steel) with a crossbrace which resembles the rungs of a wooden ladder. Each of these parts clearly embodies its individual task within the overall functional interplay.

The Castiglioni brothers consider an object to be successful when all superfluous elements have been removed, and the object has been reduced to its essentials, yet lent optimal formal expression.

In 1957, they presented the Mezzadro in its present-day form at the exhibition entitled "Colori e forme nella casa d'oggi" at Villa Olmo in Como, which contained pieces chosen according to these very criteria, including a Thonet bentwood chair, No. 18, and the Sella, a telephone seat.

Mezzadro first went into production in 1970, at which time it received its present name. Together with the

Castiglionis' design for a stool entitled Primate, it was the only piece from the extensive Zanotta collection on exhibit at the 1970 Milan furniture fair. PD

61

Name:	**No. 3107**
Designer:	**Arne Jacobsen**
Draft:	**1955**
Production:	**1955 to the present**
Manufacturer:	**Fritz Hansens Efa. A/S, Copenhagen, Denmark**
Measurements:	**H 77; W 52; D 51.5; seat height 44 cms**
Materials:	**formed plywood, chrome-plated tubular steel, rubber**

In the early fifties, the Danish furniture industry adopted a new manufacturing process. Solid wood was increasingly replaced by materials such as steel and plywood, significantly reducing the need for complex structures.
Arne Jacobsen's chair is an outstanding example of this newfound simplicity. It consists of only a few parts, can be produced at low cost, and is extremely lightweight. The seat and back are made up of an ordinary piece of plywood, while the arrangement and form of the three steel tube legs attached to the underside of the seat in the center enable the chair to be stacked.
Charles Eames and Eero Saarinen had already produced a three-dimensional chair shell in the few prototypes of their Organic Armchair back in 1940/41. They had tried to prevent breakage

between seat and backrest where three-dimensional distortion was the greatest by leaving a gap in the material, whereas Jacobsen approached the problem from the outside. He narrowed and reinforced the conjunction of the differently arched surfaces of seat and back by means of additional layers of veneer. This guaranteed that the backrest was both stable and flexible.

The predecessor of Jacobsen's chair, which played an important part in the modernization of Scandinavian furniture design, was given the popular epithet "Ant" owing to its characteristic curved body and the thin legs. In 1955, No. 3107 emerged, a variation featuring a less segmented waistline and four legs. This successor was available in a multitude of colors and became highly popular. PR

62

Name:	**Coconut Chair**
Designer:	**George Nelson**
Draft:	**1955**
Production:	**1956-1964**
Manufacturer:	**Herman Miller Furniture Company, Zeeland, Michigan**
Measurements:	**H 84; W 104; D 86; seat height 34 cms**
Materials:	**polished aluminum, sheet steel, foam rubber, artificial leather, chrome-plated round steel**

Like his Marshmallow sofa, Nelson's Coconut armchair also alludes to the spontaneous lifestyle of the sixties, which was shaped by everyday culture. Instead of looking for a shape functionally equivalent to the human body, Nelson made a memorable symbolic statement that introduced a new, deliberately easy-going type of sitting. He found a crucial impulse for his shapes in the expansive gestures of popular fifties art such as the abstract-surrealistic work of Joan Miró, or Alexander Calder.
In the original version, the shell looked like a coconut and consisted of a piece of bent steel with foam rubber padding available in artificial leather, fabric, or leather upholstery. The frame was made of a piece of steel tube bent along the length of the shell for the two front legs,

with a second piece for the back legs, whereby the legs which stuck out were stabilized additionally by welded crossbars. Thus, the frame seemed to stretch across a floating curved form and to be attached to the floor. Herman Miller later produced the shell using fiberglass-reinforced polyester and screwed aluminum tube legs singly onto the form; the crossbars were also screwed on. The initial production of a footstool to match the chair was later discontinued. The Coconut shown here represents a mixed form in the history of the chair, and the new frame supports a shell made of steel. Vitra has been producing the Coconut since 1988. MSC

63

Name: **Marshmallow**
Designer: **George Nelson**
Draft: **1956**
Production: **1956 - c. 1965**
Manufacturer: **Herman Miller Furniture Company, Zeeland, Michigan**
Measurements: **H 77; W 131.5; D 80; seat height 42 cms**
Materials: **varnished steel tubing, aluminum, vinyl cushions**

George Nelson is one of the most influential personalities in U.S. design after 1945. As of 1946 he was for many years head of the Design Department at the Herman Miller company, on whose behalf he engaged designers hardly known at the time, such as Charles Eames, Isamu Noguchi, and Alexander Girard. And he was also inspired by other areas of culture: alongside his work as an architect, he concerned himself with ongoing sociological and artistic themes.
Nelson's Marshmallow sofa must be considered one of the earliest Pop Art furniture designs: the transformation of a traditional sofa into a three-dimensional structure made of soft, colored cushioning. The seat and back are supported by a steel construction and the unit has the shape of an axially symmetrical folded-out waffle. Unlike

traditional upholstered sofas, it was possible to make it available in numerous colors and sizes thanks to what was at the time a completely novel, additive construction system. However, production required costly labor inputs; additionally, the unorthodox sofa hardly seemed to fit in contemporary interiors. Production at Herman Miller was therefore discontinued around 1965.

From 1988 to 1994, Vitra produced the Marshmallow sofa again. MSC

64

Name: **No. 670 and No. 671, Lounge Chair and Ottoman**
Designers: **Charles and Ray Eames**
Draft: **1956**
Production: **1956 to the present**
Manufacturer: **Herman Miller Furniture Company, Zeeland, Michigan**
Measurements: **H 82; W 83; D 84; seat height 35 cms / H 42; W 65; D 53.5 cms**
Materials: **bent plywood, rosewood veneer, blackened and polished cast aluminium, leather cushions, plastic, rubber**

Like many of the Eameses' furniture designs, the club chair No. 670 was the result of Charles Eames's cooperation with Eero Saarinen in 1940, when both participated in the New York MoMA's "Organic Design in Home Furnishings" competition. Based on the arm chair exhibited there made of a single piece of three-dimensionally shaped plywood for the seat and back, Eames Office prototypes were created in 1946 using three separate bent plywood elements for shoulders, back, and seat; these were connected by hard rubber discs. Tubular steel and plywood structures were tried out as supports. Don Albinson, who had worked with Eames

since 1946, was involved in these earlier experiments as well as on the final version shown here, which was created ten years later.
Although it can be easily and completely dismantled using only a monkey wrench, the construction of the chair is more complex than any other chair designed by Charles and Ray Eames. Moreover, it is the most comfortable and most expensive piece of furniture the couple created. The plywood shells, bent two-dimensionally for the shoulders, back, seat, and ottoman were veneered in the early version with rosewood and later with walnut or rosewood. The leather upholstery, originally filled with goosefeathers and later with soft foam, is completely removable. One special feature of the construction is the connection of the seat to the back. While both back sections are held together by two cast aluminum supports and hard rubber discs, the armrests provide the only connection of the back with the shell and feature washers made of Neoprene. The chair can be rotated on the star-base, but its individual elements are firmly connected to each other. Its inviting soft padding and the generous, well-shaped dimensions offer, at least in conjunction with the ottoman, nearly optimal sitting comfort. The Eameses' "Lounge Chair," taking its cue from the club chairs of the last century, owes its striking appearance first to its impressive size, which gently embraces the user. Also worth mentioning are the high-grade materials; even the aluminum is enhanced by expensive finishing on the polished outer side and blackened side parts. At the same time, the division between the individual functions through the

segmentation of the structure and the use of different materials gives the chair a technical appearance. This linking of a technically mature modern structure with luxurious sitting comfort soon turned the chair into a beloved (and expensive) status symbol. In 1957 it was awarded first prize at the Triennial in Milan. Far more than 100,000 of this model have been produced to date by Herman Miller, and after 1958 also by Vitra, and the chair is considered one of the great design classics. MSC

65

Name:	**No. 151, Tulip Chair**
Designer:	**Eero Saarinen**
Draft:	**1956**
Production:	**1956 to the present**
Manufacturer:	**Knoll Associates, Inc., New York**
Measurements:	**H 80,5; W 49,5; D 54; seat height 48 cms**
Materials:	**varnished fiberglass-reinforced polyester, varnished cast aluminum, foam rubber, textile**

The Tulip Chair is one of a series of chairs, armchairs, stools, tables, and side tables developed by Eero Saarinen within a five-year period. The characteristic feature of the series is that the supporting structure has been pared to a central supporting stem "like a wineglass" in order to emphasize the uniformity of table and chair. "The bases of tables and chairs in a typical furniture arrangement create an ugly, confusing, and restless world. I wanted to design a chair as an integrated whole once again. All important furniture of the past always had a holistic structure, from King Tut's chair to that of Thomas Chippendale. Today, we are parting ways with this holism with our predilection for plastic and laminated wood shells. In current production methods, pedestal furniture is half plastic and half metal.

I am looking forward to the point when the plastics industry will be capable of manufacturing the chair using just one material, the way I have designed it." The Tulip Chair is still produced today in its original form. PD

66

Name:	**K 3**
Designer:	**Verner Panton**
Draft:	**1958**
Production:	**1959-1964**
Manufacturers:	**Plus Linje, Copenhagen**
Measurements:	**H 90; W 99.5; D 60.5 cms**
Materials:	**sheet steel, foam rubber, woolen covers**

The first Scandinavian designer to break radically with the Scandinavian tradition of working with solid woods was Verner Panton, a Dane who opted for unusual, colorful designs for furniture, materials and everyday appliances. In the 1960s, he became a veritable trend-setter in European design in the 1960s.
In 1958, Panton, who was essentially an architect, was commissioned to design the extension for the Komigen Kro restaurant on the Danish island of Fünen. While the design for the annex, with its reliance on concrete, wood and glass, was somewhat restrained, the furnishing of the restaurant provoked all the more excitement as all of them, from curtains via tablecloths, walls and lamps right through to the furniture were in red. For a part of the furniture, Panton designed a series of tables and revolving chairs based on an upside-down cone and called Cone Chairs as they resembled ice-cream cones. A local craftsman produced about 25-30 of them for the restaurant, and they were likewise covered in red.
The same year, Plus Linje was founded to market

Panton's drafts. While Panton worked on further models of the Cone Chairs, the furniture for the Komigen Kro restaurant went on show at the large furniture trade fair in Fredericia in Denmark. Again, Panton lived up to his reputation as an imaginative designer, for he positioned the furniture on the ceiling, affording the hordes of visitors a better view of the items. In 1959, Plus Linje finally launched production of an entire series, which included not only the simple Cone Chairs and tables for Komigen Kro, but also additional variants, among other things the model shown here, with its doubly curved back.

As with many of Panton's designs, the Cone Chairs catch the eye especially thanks to their idiosyncratic construction, which appears to contradict the laws of gravity since the entire weight is concentrated on the connecting point between cone and base. Thanks to the load-bearing feet and their stable anchorage in the interior of the cone, the chair is sufficiently stable and rigid. This balancing act of vectors running together at one point is especially pronounced in K 3, a chair also nicknamed "Mickey Mouse" or "Bat" owing to the curved back. Although with its organic form, the K 3 reveals influences from the world of the applied arts in the 1950s, like the entire series it also anticipates important elements of the colorful and bold Pop Art aesthetics of the 1960s.

While Plus Linje discontinued production of K 3 in 1964, followed a little later by the other Cone Chairs, in the 1980s Fritz Hansen included the wire version of the Cone chair in its collection. Since 1994, Polythema, a

German company, has started making K 3 and the simple Cone Chair again, albeit in a slightly altered version using acrylic glass or leather. MK

67

Name:	**Indoor-Outdoor Reclining Armchair No. 684, Alu Chair**
Designers:	**Charles and Ray Eames**
Draft:	**1958**
Production:	**1958 to the present**
Manufacturer:	**Herman Miller Furniture Company, Zeeland, Michigan**
Measurements:	**H 100; W 65; D 77; seat height 40 cms**
Materials:	**polished and clear-coated cast aluminum, synthetic fiber**

The Alu Chair stems from a suggestion by Alexander Girard and Eero Saarinen who were looking for suitable furniture for a house they had just completed for Irvin Miller. Girard, who as an architect was also interested in horticulture and was the director for textile production at Herman Miller, complained that although contemporary furnishings existed for inside, there was no good-looking terrace or garden furniture. Charles Eames could not get this idea out of his head, and he tried to help his friend. During an airplane flight, he thought of the idea of material stretched across an aluminum frame construction.

Even prior to that Eames had intended to produce metal furniture (in 1948 using embossed aluminum for the New York Museum of Modern Art competition "Low-Cost

Furniture Design" or in 1951 using welded wire for the Wire Chairs). Again he wanted to develop a body-shaped form, not as a hard shell but as an elastic length of material between the side pieces which followed the body contours. He sketched the profile of the sides on the back of an envelope. The material was reinforced on the side by means of a narrow strip of plastic and was fixed in a groove turned to the outside. After returning from his trip, his former student at the Cranbrook Academy of Art and then colleague, Don Albinson, began immediately with the construction of wood models of the profile and the crossbeams or stretcher. It was soon decided that a symmetrical arrangement of the grooves in a double T-beam configuration would be more stable. The inner groove could then serve as an opening for the crossbeams and thus the right and left profile would be identical (except for the drilling); thereafter, all that remained was to develop the side sections. The synthetic fiber Saran, developed by Alexander Girard and the Eames Office in four colors, seemed to be appropriate for use outdoors, and triple layers of the fiber were stretched between the sides, overlapping in the spots where the seat, back, and headrest would be subject to the greatest wear and tear. Unfortunately their expectations with regard to the material were sadly dashed, for it soon rotted when left outside. Saran had to be replaced by a heat-sealed artificial leather, called Koroseal or Naugahide.

Further experiments led to a padded sandwich construction featuring two layers of Naugahide with a thin padding of vinyl foam and vinyl padding which was "quilted" every 1 7/8 inches by high-frequency welding, which lent the "Aluminum Group" chairs and armchairs the look they have today. Originally developed for outdoors, the first mass-produced aluminum chairs and armchairs are now only used indoors and as classics have not lost any of their modernity. PD

68

Name:	**Lambda**
Designers:	**Marco Zanuso, Richard Sapper**
Draft:	**1959-1964**
Production:	**1964**
Manufacturer:	**Gavina s.p.a., Bologna**
Measurements:	**H 77.5; W 39.5; D 46; seat height 44 cms**
Materials:	**stamped steel, varnished; rubber**

Marco Zanuso is considered the great rationalist of postwar Italian design. In 1939 he took a degree in architecture at the Milan Polytechnic and opened his own office in 1945. Between 1958 and 1977 he collaborated closely with Richard Sapper.

Zanuso dedicated himself intensively to material analysis and technology research. In 1959 he received a contract for the development of a low-cost kitchen chair whose seat and back should be made out of plastic; his client gave him complete design freedom in creating the connections of the parts and the shape of the base.

After producing numerous prototypes, Zanuso disregarded the original specifications and developed an all-metal chair. One of these trial models was awarded the silver medal of the XII Milan Triennial.

He envisioned mass-production as in the automobile industry and was involved with preliminary technological studies over the course of five years.

The Lambda consists of a total of ten stamped, thin sheets of metal, which could also be shaped and assembled by small metalworking shops. The seat shell has a double-walled construction. In the space inbetween the seat and back sections, the inner and outer form differ from each other to the greatest degree, thus creating the greatest hollow space. This increases the stability. The four U-shaped folded legs blend with the inner shell and are securely connected with the outer shell by curved gussets. All connections are electrically spot-welded together. At the end of the process, the chair is sprayed in high-gloss paint.
This particular construction affords a great degree of stability despite the use of a thin material and its minimal weight. The fold of the legs predates the later style of low-cost plastic garden chairs. Unlike these, the "Lambda" cannot be stacked. A later version was planned with a leather pad which was to be glued into the shell.
Despite the already mentioned advantages, it still was not possible for Zanuso to succeed in automating production. Since the individual parts had to be assembled by hand, the expected high unit output was not achieved. The design was discontinued after the trial series. PD

69

Name:	**Panton Chair**
Designer:	**Verner Panton**
Draft:	**1959/60**
Production:	**1968 to the present**
Manufacturer:	**Herman Miller AG/ Vitra AG, Basel**
Measurements:	**H 88.5; W 50; D 74; seat height 43 cms**
Materials:	**varnished high-resistance foam (Baydur)**

Danish designer Verner Panton is one of the group of designers who broke with the Scandinavian tradition of producing handcrafted teak wood furniture. He shares this distinction with Poul Kjaerholm and Arne Jacobsen, in whose architecture studio he worked from 1950-1952.

As early as 1949/50, Panton began drafting chairs with no rear legs during his studies at the Royal Academy of Art in Copenhagen. In 1955 a chair emerged that was made of molded laminated wood and featured one unbroken S-curve; it was part of an entire furniture line. However, Panton was fascinated by the opportunities opened up by the new plastics, which, due to their lack of structure, do not limit the designer to any particular forms, and engender inexpensive products. This new formal freedom caused him to reconsider the theme "chair," and he again returned to the S-chair and modified it. The

crucial feature was the curved lower part, which rendered the base of the S-chair superfluous and afforded the desired leg room.
At the end of the fifties, together with Dansk Acrylic Teknik, he developed the prototype for the Panton Chair in plastic and exhibited it at the Mobilia-Club on Eriksholm, near Helsingör, in the hope of finding a suitable manufacturer with whom he could realize his idea. He found none and the cantilever-base plastic chair initially remained a dream. Panton returned again to working with laminated wood.
In 1962/63 he paid a visit to Vitra. Only after making contact with the owners Willi and Rolf Fehlbaum, who manufactured Herman Miller products under license, did years of experimentation finally yield the first fiberglass-reinforced polyester prototypes in 1967. However, the desire to make the Panton Chair stackable once again delayed production, as the thickness of the material had to be reduced without forfeiting stability.
The final version went into serial production in 1968 at Vitra under the label of the Herman Miller Furniture Co. It was made of Baydur, an HR polyurethane foam produced by the Bayer Leverkusen company, and was varnished in seven colors. The Panton Chair was thus the first product developed jointly by Vitra and Bayer Leverkusen to be included in the Herman Miller collection. It quickly won fame and became a Pop Art icon.
In 1970 Vitra replaced the costly production technology, which required thirty minutes to produce

one piece, with Thermoplast injection molding. Using a dyed granulate Luran-S made by BASF, the edge profiles had to be strengthened and reinforcing ribs placed underneath the seat.

In the long run, however, the material did not adequately withstand dynamic stress; Vitra discontinued production in 1979 and the license was returned to Verner Panton. Starting in 1983, Horn GmbH & Co. KG in Rudersberg began making the chair using HR foam again, and sold it until the end of the eighties through the WK association. Since 1990 Vitra has been producing the Panton Chair using HR foam.

The colorful history of the first serially produced cantilever-base chair made of one single piece of plastic includes numerous quarrels as to the true designer. Because Panton had unsuccessfully sought a manufacturer for quite some time, he had already made his ideas available to a limited audience despite the fact that mass production did not seem imminent. When the Panton Chair finally went into serial production, many other designers claimed they had also pursued this idea, although without taking steps to publicize it, have it serially produced, or obtain a patent. PD

I like small objects in big spaces because they become bigger than life.

Bob Wilson, Opera Director, 1997

Rowland
Belotti
Colombo
Gruppo Strum
Aarnio
Piretti
Pesce
Archizoom

7

1961-1970

Consumption and Protest

The boom in industry and commerce also continues in the early 1960s. In some European countries, there were even labor shortages so that foreign workers from southern Europe had to be recruited. In the Western industrialized countries, a saturation point had been reached, with the lion's share of households already equipped with the most important technical appliances. Nevertheless, demand is bolstered through **advertising** and short-lived products. The contents and motifs of **consumer society** become the object of artistic creation. While the champions of **Pop Art** copy cans and ad symbols, thus casting doubt on the contrast between art and triviality, pop groups like the **Beatles** become the idols of young people aspiring to prosperity. The first successes in **space travel** spawn visions of space travel through the universe which are reflected in film and fashion, but also in furniture design.

While the increasing criticism of the ruling social system culminates in the **student unrest** and the **Hippie movement**, a change in furniture design looms as early as the early 1960s. The reason: not only a change in ideas, but above all the increase in technological and design possibilities generated by the use of plastics. While some designers continue to strive to tap the economic advantages of plastics, others also recognize the creative potential of this material. The fact that plastic can almost be molded and colored at will

spawned a trend toward organically rounded, seamless shapes which appear to have been molded in one piece. **Verner Panton** (66, 69), a Dane, succeeds in designing a chair that is formed out of only one piece of plastic. The most influential personalities of the day also include **Joe Colombo** (73), who drafts both innovative mass products in an individual and consistent idiom and futuristic spatial scenarios.
As of about 1965, groups such as **Archizoom Associati** (78), **Studio 65** (80) or **Gruppo Strum** (74) cause a stir with Utopian architectural projects, experimental furniture designs and happenings. They endeavor to present alternatives to the strict separation of pre-defined spaces, to rationalistic, rectangular architecture and items of furniture which constrain and isolate the user.
The notion of living in communes found a counterpart in colorful **residential landscapes** assembled from organically formed upholstery elements that do their best to avoid interpersonal delimitation. It now became possible to create unusual, sculptural furniture using **polyurethane foam** which can be generated in a free, soft form and is stable without any internal support. Moreover, with wit, the novel **inflatable furniture is** not only provocative, but also charming with its combination of material and structure. The diversity of experiments reveal the influences of Pop and Op Art, as well as comic motifs, ecstatic states and rock music.
Simultaneously, the first traces of a nascent **Post-modernism** emerge specifically in the domain of architecture; the foundations for it are laid by US

architect **Robert Venturi** (88) in 1966 with his essay on "Complexity and Contradiction in Architecture". Instead of consistently aspiring to innovate, which was a hallmark of all Modernism, Venturi propagated **eclecticism**, which consciously avoids existing styles and traditions.

70

Name:	**40/4**
Designer:	**David Rowland**
Draft:	**approx. 1959-1964**
Production:	**as of 1964**
Manufacturers:	**GF Office Furniture Ltd. Youngstown, Ohio; Howe Europe, Middelfart, Denmark**
Measurements:	**H 76; W 49; D 54; seat height 45 cms**
Materials:	**round steel, chrome-plated, bent sheet steel with plastic covers, plastic gliders**

David Rowland, an American designer, worked from 1952-1954 in the office of Norman Bel Geddes, the most famous advocate of streamlined designs; as of 1954, he went freelance. As early as the 1950s he began to work on a design for a stackable chair to be made of thin steel rods. Rowland hoped that this method would enable him to stack chairs up to as much as four foot high (122 cm). Although Edgar Kaufmann Jr., the then director of the Design Department of the Museum of Modern Art in New York, tried to persuade him to abandon the idea, as there was ostensibly no market for such a product, Rowland persisted. He experimented for several years, creating a stackable chair: it was possible to stack up to 40 of them, with a total height of four feet

and which Rowland therefore named the 40/4. A comparison illustrates the true impact of Rowland's idea: with a frame made of tubular steel tube in the usual diameter of 25 mm, a stack of 40 chairs would be 1.76 m high and no longer movable.
Despite the filigree frame only 11 mm in diameter, the gliders ensure that the 40/4 is sufficiently stable. The seat and back-rest blend elegantly with the frame and are very comfortable thanks to their generous, ergonomic shapes; given the minimalist nature of the furniture, these qualities are far from self-evident. The chairs can even be hooked up in rows by means of flat metal connectors on the back legs.
Although today the 40/4 is one of the best-selling and most imitated chairs, Rowland had a tough time finding a manufacturer prepared to produce his design. Numerous firms turned it down and it was not until 1964 that he managed to persuade a manufacturer to take it on. An architectural office to whom Rowland had presented the chair, required a large number of chairs to furnish a university campus, and the 40/4 appeared to fit the bill perfectly. They suggested that Rowland approach the General Fireproofing Company as a possible maker, and the latter immediately took on the project; in fact, in the very first year as many as 20,000 units were manufactured. The same year, 40/4 won one of the most prestigious design prizes, the Gran Premio at the Milan Triennial, and it has since won many other awards.
The General Fireproofing Company, and with it Howe, a Danish company that held the European license, also brought to market versions the 40/4 for private use that

therefore did not feature the connectors.
The frame of the models on offer today is either chrome-plated or laminated, the seat and back-rest are made of plywood, upholstered metal, plastic, or, as in the original, of laminated metal, depending on the manufacturer. MK

71

Name:	**Spaghetti**
Designer:	**Giandomenico Belotti**
Draft:	**1962**
Production:	**as of 1970**
Manufacturers:	**Alias s.r.l., Grumello del Monte**
Measurements:	**H 83, W 40, D 53.5, seat height 46 cms**
Materials:	**tubular steel, PVC**

The principle of increasing the comfort afforded by a chair by means of an elastic fabric that gives occurred to Frenchman René Herbst as early as 1927: he made use of the chest expanders already on the market. In the 1950s, when there was great demand for low-price mass seating and plastic became popular, elastic straps as the seat or back-rest became increasingly wide-spread.
One of the best-known examples for this solution, as simple as it is elegant, is the so-called Spaghetti chair, which Italian designer and architect Giandomenico Belotti created in 1962 for a hotel in the Italian spa town of Marina. For outdoor use, the hotel chairs were outfitted with a fabric made of nylon cord covered in plastic, such as is also used for clothes lines. Although on its own the cord is less elastic, the dense network adapts to the shape of the user's body. For the interior of the hotel, the chairs were, however, fitted with leather straps.
Compared with the original 1962 version, a slightly

altered chair was manufactured as of 1970 by the Italian company, Baleri. In 1979, Alias took over production of the Spaghetti and, in 1980-1, added several variations to the chair and stool, namely a chair, a barstool and a stackable chair. In a further model, Belotti transferred the Spaghetti's strikingly bent struts onto a frame strongly reminiscent of the 1928 Fauteuil à dossier basculant by Le Corbusier, Pierre Jeanneret and Charlotte Perriand.
As low-priced mass furniture which can be manufactured without any great technical outlays, the Spaghetti was a best-seller in the 1980s. Although it had originated almost two decades earlier, its simple, transparent form concurred with the cool, neo-modern taste of this later era. MK

72

Name: **3-benet Skalstol**
Designer: **Hans J. Wegner**
Draft: **1963**
Production: **1963-1989**
Manufacturer: **Johannes Hansen, Copenhagen**
Measurements: **H 73.5; W 90; D 82.5 cms**
Materials: **varnished bent plywood, bent and varnished laminated birch wood**

Hans J. Wegner is considered to be an important innovator in traditional furniture design as well as a pioneer in Danish Modernity. He earned fame with his exclusive, perfectly crafted chairs, which often drew on traditional models and were made by hand.
After participating in "Low-Cost Furniture Design," the 1948 competition held by the MoMA in New York, he began working with the relatively new process of forming laminated wood, although only on a two-dimensional level. A preliminary Skalstol prototype from 1949, with its three separate shells, was probably a forerunner of the Eames's Lounge Chair from 1956. It already features the intelligent, highly stable leg construction which consists of just two pieces of laminated wood and thus saves material inputs. In 1963 Wegner manufactured another Skalstol prototype, this time with a distinctive form that could almost be called classic.

The latter chair only has three legs, and the rear leg doubles as the mounting for the backrest. Wegner tested several leg configurations with 1:5 scale models and ultimately opted for the solution which had already proven successful in 1949. He highlighted the curvature of both pieces of laminated wood visually by having the front legs extend sideways rather than forward. The distinctly raised ends of the plywood shell in combination with an extremely low center of gravity lend the chair a representative form that evokes chairs used by African rulers. Japanese tradition was the source of Wegner's idea of coating the surface with red varnish, and it often played an important role in other works, too. Wegner always saw himself as a craftsman whose foremost task was to create comfortable chairs. As the Skalstol demonstrates, a traditional notion of one's role can also yield great originality and elegance. MK

73

Name:	**No. 4867, Universale**
Designer:	**Joe Colombo**
Draft:	**1965**
Production:	**as of 1967**
Manufacturer:	**Cartel S.p.A., Binasco**
Measurements:	**H 71.5, W 42.5, D 50, seat height 43.5 cms**
Materials:	**Plastic ABS**

The designer Joe Colombo died in 1971 at the age of 41 and left behind him an oeuvre which is one of the most influential of the day. In his drafts for furniture, household objects, furnishings and technical instruments he broke radically with traditional materials and concentrated almost exclusively on using plastics. As a trained artist, Colombo strove to create rounded and geometrical forms, which appeared with their standardized structure to originate in one and the same mold - thus setting a key feature of design in the 1960s. The world of Colombo's ideas even extended to include fully equipped, self-sufficient residential worlds which are clearly indebted to notions derived from space travel and sci-fi.

One of Colombo's best-known and most successful designs was the stackable chair called Universale, which he made in 1965 for Kartell. Although the chair was already intended to be made of aluminum, its simple and plastic shape is considered the epitome of Colombo's creative use of plastics. Moreover, the chair is

light, durable and straightforward to manufacture, while also meeting the standards for high-grade industrial products.
Two years were spent developing a complicated plastic molding process to produce the seat and back-rest section - this enables the section to be manufactured in one single mechanical process. It was possible to remove the section from the mold thanks to a slit in the seat and back; initially the section was made of plastic ABS, later of polypropylene. Depending on the purpose for which the chair was intended, legs of differing lengths could be attached to this base element. With short legs, the Universale functioned as a garden chair, children's chair or as seating for waiting-rooms; with normal-length legs, it could be used in dining rooms, schools or hotels. Owing to the sides being flatter at the edges, rows of chairs could be created without leaving gaps in-between, while the tapering in the back area of the seat made it possible to stack the chairs in threes, as there was room for the legs of two additional chairs. Colombo also designed a version as a barstool with a high leg-frame, which doubled up as the base for a side-table, as well as a version for an arm-chair.
In 1969, Colombo's Universale was used as the seating in his spatial installation "Visiona I", a display which the German firm Bayer A.G. organized on the occasion of the Cologne Furniture Fair. In this futuristic spatial setting, in which the traditional combination of room and furniture was replaced by permanently fixed functional units made of plastic, the chair was the last movable item of conventional furniture. MK

74

Name:	**Pratone**
Designers:	**Gruppo Strum**
Draft:	**1966**
Production:	**1971 to the present**
Manufacturer:	**Gufram s.r.l., Balangero, Italy**
Measurements:	**H 95; W 140; D 140 cms**
Materials:	**cold-foamed polyurethane, green varnish**

Pratone (=lawn) is an allegory of a longing for nature which came to the fore during the second half of the sixties as part of the hippie protest against a glutted consumer society.
Television commercials, Pop Art, and psychedelic experiences were featured via enlargement, graphic processing, and "softening." Thus, "Pratone" confronts us as an artificial, mutant, and trivialized piece of nature, sparking feelings of curiosity and conflict in the observer. The passivity of sitting is portrayed as behavior typical of consumerism and juxtaposed to sensual, archaic aspects. Users first have to create a seat from the sculptural, cold impression given by the chair. Natural landscape has become a garden landscape, and, ultimately, an interior landscape, a domesticated playground. The fact that this playground can be enlarged as one wishes by joining together a number of Pratone elements corresponds

to the concept of community and "happenings." However, the material (green, varnished polyurethane foam) takes the yearning for nature to the point of absurdity.

It is not clear whether sitting "on the lawn" is intended as a lost idyll or should be seen ironically as an outdated utopia. This is left up to the user.

At the end of the sixties, the introduction of polyurethane foam was sensational in furniture design, although there are few pieces in which the features and effects of the materials were employed as consciously and overtly as in Pratone. The pieces that survived until today are no longer suitable for use, as the material becomes brittle and cracked with age.

Since 1986, when it was decided to limit the edition to 200 pieces, Gufram has produced sixteen Pratone chairs, selling them mainly to museums and galleries. At present, Gufram has manufactured a total of approximately sixty Pratones. MK

75

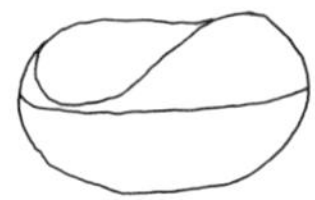

Name:	**Pastilli**
Designer:	**Eero Aarnio**
Draft:	**1967**
Production:	**as of 1967**
Manufacturer:	**Artekno Oy, Tampere, Finland**
Measurements:	**H 52, W 93 cms**
Materials:	**fiberglass**

Alongside his Ball Chair of 1963, a chair shaped like a plastic ball on a base, Pastilli, made in 1967, is one of Eero Aarnio's best-known works. The humorous quotation of a banal everyday object - which is enlarged here on an enormous scale to comprise the basic theme of this seating object - brings to mind the strategy championed by Pop Art. Aarnio uses it here in a humorous, creative approach to using plastic.
Given the rounded underside, the armchair rocks and turns pleasantly. And its low seating height corresponds to the relaxed, informal seating, as became popular in the 1960s. According to his own statements on the subject, when designing the armchair Aarnio also considered embedding it in the ball of the Ball Chair such that the two objects could be transported jointly. In addition, Aarnio emphasizes the multifunctional character of the armchair, which can also be used as a sled, a wash-basin and a water toy.
Pastilli's seemingly smooth, rounded forms are typical of the plastic furniture of the 1960s. This aesthetic resulted

among other things from the fact that it was now possible for the first time thanks to plastic, to fashion free and rounded forms almost at will and to produce them in one single manufacturing process, as if from one mold. The impression that the shape of the seat had simply been impressed on the pill-like basic body, is deceptive. In actual fact, the chair consists of two fiberglass parts, laminated by hand over a mold and then subsequently glued. MK

76

Name:	**Plia**
Designer:	**Giancarlo Piretti**
Draft:	**1968**
Production:	**1969 to the present**
Manufacturer:	**Anonima Castelli s.p.a., Ozzano, near Bologna**
Measurements:	**H 75; W 47; D 50.5; seat height 45.5 cms**
Materials:	**polished die-cast aluminum, oval tubular steel, cellidor plastic**

Lightness, flexibility, and technical precision are the obvious advantages of this design by Giancarlo Piretti. The folding mechanism of the chair was completely novel in its day. The chair rests on a joint made of three metal disks which connect the back, legs and seat in such a way that they can be folded up into a flat compact form barely five centimeters thick.
The elegant chair, which is also suitable for outdoor use, has clear rounded forms, an oval tubular steel frame, and transparent plastic surfaces. When folded up, it can be hung on a wall hook made specially for this purpose, but can also be stacked when folded out.
Due to its straightforward construction and simple manufacturing, "Plia" can be produced at low cost and offered at correspondingly favorable prices. Over four million copies have been sold since 1969. In 1971,

this exemplary design won the BIO 5 award at the Lyublyana Biennial and the Gute Form prize of the Federal Republic of Germany in 1973. PR

77

Name: UP5 and UP6, Donna
Designer: Gaetano Pesce
Draft: 1969
Production: 1970-1973
Manufacturer: C & B Italia (Cassina & Busnelli), Novedrate, near Como, Italy
Measurements: H 110; W 110; D 120; seat height 41, UP6 circumference 60 cms
Materials: polyurethane foam, cold foam-molded, nylon-jersey

Donna is completely in tune with the spirit of Pop Art and the Gaetano Pesce fondness for anthropomorphic shapes. The chair was actually designed to resemble a prehistoric, female fertility figure, with a ball attached to symbolize captivity: "In this design I have expressed my idea of women. A woman is always confined, a prisoner of herself against her will. For this reason I wanted to give this chair the shape of a woman with a ball chained to her foot to use the traditional image of a prisoner." The unconventional nature of the shape also applies to the construction and marketing of the chair which was one of a series of six. Together they succeeded in marking a radical break from traditional upholstery production thanks to the technology developed by C & B Italia for creating oversized foam parts.
Donna consists of a molded monoblock of foam without

any supporting structure since the polyurethane foam is dense and free-standing. First, a finished piece of furniture covered with elastic nylon jersey is reduced in a vacuum chamber to about 10 percent of its normal volume and is then wrapped in airtight foil. The customer can easily transport the otherwise unwieldy piece single-handedly. After removal of the wrapper at the destination, the chair slowly recovers its original shape without outside help as air seeps back into the capillaries of the polyurethane foam. PD

78

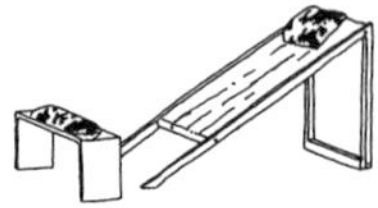

Name:	**Mies**
Designers:	**Archizoom Associati**
Draft:	**1969**
Production:	**since 1969**
Manufacturer:	**Poltronova s.r.l., Agliana, Pistoia**
Measurements:	**H 76; W 74; D 128.5 / H 30; W 104.5; D 20 cms**
Materials:	**chrome-plated steel, rubber, hide cushions**

Nineteen sixty-nine was an unusually fruitful year for formulating new ways of looking at things within the discourse on architecture and design. These can be seen as a reaction to retrospective - in other words conservative - trends in culture and society. This retrospective approach found expression in the so-called wave of nostalgia and the remake of classic Modern furniture (starting in 1962, Gavina began production of the B 3 club chair by Marcel Breuer with the popular name "Wassily," taken over by Knoll in 1969; in 1964 Cassina acquired the rights to Le Corbusier's tubular steel furniture, which went into series production starting in 1965; between 1960 and 1970, Knoll considerably expanded the Mies van der Rohe Collection). Dedicated designers saw this as an almost existential threat to the development of contemporary design, not to mention their own possibilities as designers; and they attacked unrestrained growth as a product of misdirected consumerism. In 1966 the Archizoom Associati group in Florence not only acted as a provocative antipode to the dazzling design metropolis of Milan, but also became a seedbed of Radical Design.

The Mies chair reflects the ambivalent currents of this period (i.e., resuming production of tubular steel furniture despite mounting criticism of the Bauhaus and Functionalism).

Ludwig Mies van der Rohe, the last Bauhaus director, was one of the most prominent personalities of classic Modernity. (He died on August 17, 1969.) His love for detail yielded wonderfully elegant buildings and furniture which even today retain all their fascination.

In this regard, the name of the chair can superficially be understood as a kind of tribute. On the other hand, the "Mies" chair refutes the widely cited formula of Functionalism, namely that "form follows function": The seat, made of tightly spanned latex rubber, gives the chair a wedgelike appearance when it is not in use, and thus makes it seem unfit for sitting. However, it gives elastically to the weight of the user and therefore even offers a certain degree of seating comfort, which is enhanced by the footstool.

The sharp edges of the design form a deliberate contrast to the idyllic playfulness of the indirectly illuminated footstool. The hide-covered upholstery is a reference to Le Corbusier's preference for hide as a furniture covering; a later version sports a neck-roll similar to the one made famous by his Chaise longue à réglage continu.

The members of Archizoom Associati went their separate ways in 1974, and their individual designs have also been successful. PD

I have always been interested in changing the scale of objects and using them in a paradoxical way: this is „Gulliver's game".

Alessandro Mendini, Designer, 1997

Castiglioni
Studio 65
Mari
Gehry
Colani
Lange
Mendini
Wewerka
Bellini
Venturi

8

1971-1980

An Obituary to Modernism

Social unrest in the late 1960s did not lead to a complete upheaval, but did provide numerous new stimuli to thought. The strategy of nuclear deterrence and the **Cold War** keep the ideological debate going, while in 1972 the Club of Rome is the first major body to draw attention to the **ecological dangers** resulting from the exploitation of nature. The same year, an important exhibition in the New York Museum of Modern Art entitled **"Italy: The New Domestic Landscape"** attests to the international import of Italian design and helps popularize its unorthodox ideas. However, the **oil crisis** of 1973 shatters any faith in progress and effectively sweeps away plastic furniture, until then the epitome of modern design. Untroubled experimentation gives way to a holistic approach which tackles ecological, industrial production processes and products.

The cardboard furniture series Easy Edges created by the architect **Frank O. Gehry** (81, 98) earns praise as a meaningful alternative to plastic furniture. Gehry's method can be used to manufacture free, imaginative forms out of cardboard, which, at the same time, can easily be disposed of by means of **recycling**.

Gaetano Pesce (77, 92), an Italian designer, was a product of the radical Italian design movement around the groups Archizoom Associati or Superstudio, which had given birth to provocative, socially Utopian projects in the late 1960s and early 1970s. He set out to identify innovative production processes which allowed industrial mass production, on the one hand, and unmistakably individual objects, on the other, thanks to **diversification**. Pesce's highly personal aesthetics is also reminiscent of the works of the **Art Povera** movement.

Italians **Paolo Deganello** (78) and **Enzo Mari** (85) are less experimental, but their design works are likewise **conceptual**. In some of his designs, Deganello tried to structure the production process for his furniture such that the individual components were manufactured by different makers or made of industrial semi-finished parts, thus lowering investment costs for the maker of the final product. This concept can also be seen in the unorthodox, collage-like shape of many of his drafts. Mari, by contrast, subordinates any aesthetic requirements to his responsibility as a designer of socially meaningful products.

Designs by the **Alchimia** group founded in 1976 adhere to the principle of "**new craftsmanship**", although this does not exclude the use of highly developed technologies. In contrast to the avant-garde's attempts, which react with new ideas to the changed circumstances, **Alchimia** takes an essentially post-modern approach and opts more for aesthetically-artistic goals. The pioneer of the group is **Alessandro Mendini** (84) , who champions an idiom composed of quotations from historical styles, banal everyday objects and **kitsch**, while at the same time emphasizing intellectual and mystical aspects of the design process. The view that the avant-garde is itself out of date and formally new designs are no longer possible, also comes to the fore in Mendini's **re-design** work, in which he revises famous furniture by earlier designers, and ornaments them with decorations.

79

Name:	**No. 24 (No. 240), Primate**
Designer:	**Achille Castiglioni**
Draft:	**1970**
Production:	**1970**
Manufacturer:	**Zanotta S.p.A. Nova Milanese**
Measurements:	**H 50, W 82, D 46.5, knee-height 30 cms**
Materials:	**polystyrene, chrome-plated tubular steel, imitation leather, polyurethane foam**

In 1944, Achille Castiglioni joined the architectural office of his brothers Livio and Pier Giacomo; as of 1968 he worked freelance as an architect, designer, exhibition designer and lecturer. With his innovative, expedient drafts, he is considered a pioneer of modern industrial design.
Primate, a squat chair, illustrates Castiglioni's ability to fully re-define an object by analyzing its functional and ergonomic characteristics. Instead of opting for the usual subdivision of a chair into back, seat and legs, he develops a fully new type of seating, consisting of a large padded section for the knees, a tubular steel connector and a small seating cushion. Castiglioni himself says that the brief was for a chair that used a minimum of space and simultaneously guaranteed maximum freedom of movement. Primate, an unorthodox solution to this task, makes a seating posture possible which has precious

little in common with the West European seating tradition, but rather takes up the Oriental tradition of crouching relaxed close to the ground. By simply shifting some of the body weight from the seat onto the knees, the spine is relieved and stomach muscles relaxed. This squatting position led to the shape coming to be known as a squat chair.

Primate was presented at the Milan Furniture Fair in 1970 along with Mezzadro, a stool designed back in 1957, in the new Zanotta program. The fair exhibit was a prototype with a black tubular steel element and a brown knee pad, reminiscent of the surface structure of a ribbed beetle's carapace. The upholstery of the series-produced model uses more straightforward stitching and consists of leather or Vistram plastic, while the connector is made of chrome-plated tubular steel.

In 1984, Primate was part of a Castiglioni installation at the Tokyo "Mobili Italiani" show. Here, Castiglioni placed one squat chair each in front of his own Cumano café tables, arranging several of these units in a semicircle. As a counterweight to this striking sub-division into individual sets, the Primate had an integrative function, for, bereft of arm or back-rests, it does not separate the user from the surrounding space and his fellow men.

Since the late 1970s, numerous items of seating are on the market that take their cue from the principle used in Castiglioni's Primate. MK

80

Name:	**Capitello**
Designers:	**Studio 65**
Draft:	**1971**
Production:	**1971**
Manufacturers:	**Gufram s.r.l., Balangero, Italy**
Measurements:	**H 78; W 110; D 120 cms**
Materials:	**Polyurethane foam**

Studio 65, a group of designers and architects, was founded in Turin in 1965. In 1971, it had approx. 15 members who focused on experimental architecture, furniture and graphic work, combining elements from Pop Art, advertising and the hippie movement to forge an eclectic idiom linking kitsch and art.

Among the group's furniture designs, usually involving polyurethane foam, a series of sculptural furniture stands out in particular; it was were produced along with drafts by other designers as a limited edition entitled "Multipli" by Gufram. The "Multipli" fully and radically exploit the design scope afforded by cold-foamed polyurethane, since this makes the traditional construction of furniture superfluous. In the process, the furniture displays stylistic features which stemmed from the fine arts of the 1960s: the soft sculptures by Claes Oldenburg, a naive stylization taken from the comic and ad drawings or the almost trance-like out-sized dimensions of the objects.

Alongside a lip-like sofa, a cactus-shaped clothes horse and a Babylonian temple as a toy system for children,

Studio 65's contribution to the series included a chair in the form of the capital of a Greek column, aptly named Capitello, produced in a limited edition of 200. Studio 65 wrote the following on it:

"The past does not belong us[...] We are only "practicing architects", and all that we know of the past or all that interests us in it is that which still strides toward us from the past[...]

If this living object, with its titled back head, this mother's breast that has become a sofa, is even remotely similar to an Ionic capital, then the reasons for this are obvious.

Is it perhaps a left-over Ionic capital on the Acropolis, on which a tourist exhausted by photographing has sat down? [...]

Is it a capital made of plastic and quartz sand, such as one finds in a souvenir shop? [...]

Is it a capital from a book on architectural history? [...]

Is it a capital which I have seen engraved on a book cover, in the study of an old judge?

Or is it perhaps the superimposition all of these pictures, which have sedimented in consciousness, which produce a new, enlarged object, bereft of all possible functions from the past, projected into a different context, signs of a purely critical consciousness?"

The motive of the Greek column as the epitome of the monumental and of historical tradition, fragmented and placed in a new significative context, was a leitmotif in the works of Studio 65 in the early 1970s. In addition to a further chair in the form of a sloped column for the "Multipli" series, Studio 65 integrated the motif into trade fair buildings and poster designs, setting an out-sized column pedestal on the roof of a shopping center. MK

81

Name: **Wiggle Side Chair**
Designer: **Frank O. Gehry**
Draft: **1972**
Production: **1972**
Producer: **Easy Edges, Inc., New York**
Measurements: **H 85; W 42.5; D 60; seat height 45.5 cms**
Materials: **corrugated cardboard, fiberboard, round timber**

Cardboard furniture came on the scene during the sixties as a cheap and light alternative to traditional furniture. At that time attempts were made to reinforce the support the single-layer cardboard offered by using folds, tabs, slots, and other devices. Nevertheless, cardboard was not able to compete against plastic, which was just as light.

Frank O. Gehry discovered a process that ensured cardboard furniture-making a new burst of popularity. "One day I saw a pile of corrugated cardboard outside of my office - the material which I prefer for building architecture models - and I began to play with it, to glue it together and to cut it into shapes with a hand saw and a pocket knife." It was thus possible to transform massive blocks of cardboard into cardboard sculptures.

Gehry named this material Edge Board: it consisted of glued layers of corrugated cardboard running in alternating directions, and in 1972 he introduced a series of cardboard furniture under the name Easy

Edges. The Easy Edges were extraordinarily sturdy, and due to their surface quality, had a noise-reducing effect in a room. The design theorist Victor Papanek, one of the first to address the ecological responsibility of designers, praised Edge Board as a useful application of a packing material to furniture. The Easy Edges were a great success and brought Gehry overnight fame as a furniture designer, but at the same time he was into a role he did not like. Even sales prices were no longer consistent with Gehry's basic idea of offering furniture to suit anyone's pocketbook. "I started to feel threatened. I closed myself off for weeks at a time in a room to rethink my life. I decided that I was an architect, not a furniture designer ... and I simply stopped doing it."
Gehry made an international breakthrough as an architect in the late seventies, among other things with the design for his private residence in Santa Monica, California, in 1978. Since 1986 Vitra AG has reproduced four models of his Easy Edges. MK

82

Name:	**Sitzgerät Colani**
Designer:	**Luigi Colani**
Draft:	**1972**
Production:	**1973-1982**
Manufacturer:	**Top System Burkhard Lübke, Gütersloh, Germany**
Measurements:	**H 65.5; W 54; D 66; seat height 38 cms**
Materials:	**Polyethylene (rotation sintering procedure)**

The Zocker for children and the Sitzgerät Colani (Colani seating tool) strikingly reflect changes in living conditions and ways of life at the end of the sixties and the beginning of the seventies. The general acceptance of the new plastics also meant that new shapes were finding their way into apartments, often in the Pop and "shock" colors typical of the period.
Luigi Colani, who was facetiously referred to as "Leonardo of the Plastics," had for quite some time been taking advantage of the ease with which plastic could be formed into almost any shape to realize his novel drafts.
In designing the Zocker chair for children, Colani completely broke with tradition by refusing to create a scaled-down version of an adult's chair. Typologically speaking, the Zocker consists of an integrated seat and desk. It offers several sitting positions - including

straddling - and thus permits the child to move freely while playing.

The rounded edges and the smooth transitions between the seat, backrest, and desk reduce the risk of injury and ensure that the furniture is stable and stackable. In addition, the plastic is easy to clean and is shock- and scratch-resistant. Its light weight makes it mobile and even buoyant.

The numerous advantages of the child's version inspired Colani to create the Sitzgerät Colani" a chair for adults; here, the monolithic Zocker design was replaced by a sleeker, more differentiated form. What both models share is their multifunctionality, which led Colani to consider orthopedic aspects: "A person sitting in a relaxed position, leaning forward slightly, will support the shoulders above the elbows in such a way as to relieve pressure on the spine. I created a mold of the cavities formed by the human body in this position and stylistically turned them into a seating machine."[18] Characteristic of Colani's works are their highly functional properties, although they feature an organic, dynamic, biomorphic formal language that promotes ergonomic aspects. The latest design trends appear to use Colani's idiom. PD

83

Name:	**No. 2200, Flex**
Designer:	**Gerd Lange**
Draft:	**1974**
Production:	**as of 1976**
Manufacturers:	**Gebr. Thonet AG, Frankenberg**
Measurements:	**H 79; W 49; D 49; seat height 46.5 cms**
Materials:	**Beechwood, plywood, polypropylene**

Flex, a chair created in 1974 by German designer Gerd Lange, was the first chair partially made of plastic included in the program marketed by Thonet, the famous bentwood and tubular steel furniture manufacturers. While plastic seating elements had traditionally been fastened to metal frames, such as in the designs of Charles Eames, Lange combined this material with a frame made of beech wood. This hitherto unusual choice of materials and the solid appearance set the Flex clearly off from the refined metal and plastic furniture which had arisen in the context of the modern steel and glass architecture.
Seat and back-rest are composed of a single piece of plastic, which is strengthened under the seat with parallel ridges and tapers toward the rear; as a consequence, there is sufficient space to stack several chairs. During assembly, the plastic element is simply stuck simply on the front and rear legs, which have been

joined together beforehand by plywood sides. Apart from this elegant visual form generated by the beautifully emphasized connectors between the two components, the slotting process also makes ecological sense, since the two components of the chair can easily be separated and recycled.
In a similarly simple way, the basic Flex model can be expanded at will. A hood locks the upper end of the fixture for the rear legs and can be opened in order to insert various functional extensions. Thus, an arm-rest bent at right angles can be fastened between this fixture and the hole in the side of the plywood parts; the arm-rest can, in turn, be outfitted with a writing or reading rest. Flex can be connected in rows; the small or large connector is simply hooked into the side sections and serves as a rest. The variable chair system is rounded out by a small table. MK

84

Name:	**Sedia Spaziale**
Designer:	**Alessandro Mendini**
Draft:	**1975**
Production:	**1975**
Manufacturers:	**Studio Alchimia, Milan**
Measurements:	**H 85, W 55, D 56.5, seat height 48 cms**
Materials:	**wood, hammer-gray enamel, rubber covering**

In Alessandro Mendini's oeuvre as a designer, author, artist and architect, design-related, theoretical and journalistic elements blend. In 1974-5, Mendini brought together his views on the intellectual and associative substance of furniture in a series of "Mini monuments to spiritual use". As editor-in-chief of the Casabella magazine from 1970-5, he drafted parts of this series as title-page designs; this was also the case with Sedia Spaziale. Issue No. 399 dating from 1975 shows drawings of this chair and the pertinent table, like celestial objects floating in empty space.
Formally, Sedia Spaziale follows after the Lassú chair which Mendini burnt in a happening outside the editorial offices of Casabella to emphasize the ritual character of the object. Given that Lassú was, however, completely enthroned on a conical base and thus Sedia Spaziale constitutes a domesticated version of it. In the associative world of Mendini's "Mini monuments to spiritual use", Sedia Spaziale emphasizes the futuristic aspects of the

chair, whereas the burnt Lassú stressed the archaic aspects. Mendini explains the idea behind the Sedia Spaziale as follows:
"The cosmic character of these objects is derived from the appearance of satellites, with their broad bases, the way they mirror what is below them, the disproportional elements and the impression of weightlessness."
In the workshop of Studio Alchimia, the design group founded in 1976, and Mendini was its most important intellectual pioneer since joining in 1977, at intervals, four chairs and a table were manufactured in line with Mendini's drawings. In 1978, he put them on show in the spatial installation "Stanza del Secolo" ("Room of the Century") in Ferrara and then, in 1981, in the "Stanza da Manuale" ("Room of Handcraftsmanship") in Bologna. In the process, he combined them with other designs he had created to form an eclectic interior, in which in Mendini's typical way, the trivial, the historical, the fantastic and the artistic blend to form a post-modern collage of images. MK

85 

Name:	**Box**
Designer:	**Enzo Mari**
Draft:	**1976**
Production:	**1976-1995**
Manufacturers:	**Anonima Castelli s.p.a., Ozzano / Bologna**
Measurements:	**H 83; W 44.5; D 46.5; seat height 46 cms**
Materials:	**PVC-coated tubular steel, polypropylene**

Enzo Mari is known as a designer, theorist, artist and writer and is considered a representative of a strictly rationalist designs. In the conviction that studying social and political relationships forms the basis for all creative work, the self-professed left-winger exhibited his work at the epoch-making "Italy: The New Domestic Landscape" in the Museum of Modern Art in 1972, but did not put any practical work on who, but instead a programmatic essay.

The chair box which Mari created in 1976 for Castelli illustrates his goal of using high-tech processes to streamline the production process. The seat of the chair is composed of a piece of perforated plastic stabilized on all four sides by a chamber system with vertical walls. The perforations and chamber system keep the weight and the material inputs to a minimum. The complex plastic parts require technically demanding injection molding, so that the chair could only be sold a

reasonable price if a high number of units were produced.
Moreover, costs were also lowered by reducing the number of components to only four: the seat, back, legs and the connectors for the back-rest; this simplified the production process. Further transport and assembly costs were cut by ensuring that the buyer and not the factory was responsible for final assembly of the components. The box was delivered in a plastic bag as space-saving packaging, with the legs and back-rest stowed away in the cavity under the seat. Assembly by the buyer was conceivably simple, since only the legs and the connectors for the back-rest (made of PVC-coated steel rods) had to be screwed into the plastic seat. MK

86

Name:	**B 1**
Designer:	**Stefan Wewerka**
Draft:	**1976**
Production	**as of 1979**
Manufacturers:	**Tecta, Lauenförde**
Measurements:	**H 74, W 63,5 D 44,5, seat height 45 cms**
Materials:	**Wood, fabric cover**

Stefan Wewerka, a German architect, first caught the public eye in the 1960s with his artistic furniture installations and architecture processes. He created alienated, distorted, dissected and collaged chairs in order to generate new meanings and perspectives. Thus, for instance, in 1965 he created the slumping rubber chair or his 1971 entire classroom with chairs slanting submissively in one direction.

In 1976, taking one of his chair collages, Wewerka for the first time developed an industrial product ready to be manufactured. He took a chair split the seat in the middle at the front, while sawing a second at the side, subsequently nailing the two unequal halves together in an approximately right angle. When advancing the prototype further, Wewerka replaced the angle between the backs of the two chairs by a curve, correspondingly rounding the rear end of the seat and was thus able to dispense with the fourth, back leg.

Although the result is asymmetrical seating, which departs from the traditional typology of chairs which was

geared to the human anatomy, it affords a multitude of new possible uses, for it unites the different possible seating positions of the two underlying chairs. The back can either be used as an arm-rest, as a back-rest are used or as a writing rest and enables a relaxed position for concentrated work. Since 1979, the chair is manufactured under the designation B1 by Tecta.
Some of Wewerka's other designs, for example a fanned table or his cantilever chair, rest on the principle of asymmetry. With his search for new forms of expression and forms of functions, Wewerka inspired a young generation of German furniture designer who then breathed life into the design scene in the 1980s. MK

87

Name:	**Cab, No. 412**
Designer:	**Mario Bellini**
Draft:	**1976**
Production:	**1977 to present**
Manufacturer:	**Cassina s.p.a., Meda/Milan**
Measurements:	**H 81; W 51.5; D 46; seat height 44 cms**
Materials:	**tubular steel, butted leather cover, plastic**

Bellini's Cab essentially consists of two elements that are completely distinct. A leather cover is stretched over a bare tubular steel chair frame like a tight skin. The cover can be opened or closed via four zippers running along the inside of the legs under the seat. The only reinforcement to the structure is a plastic plate which supports the seat. The innovation here consists in Bellini's applying the principle of mounting the cover onto the frame of the metal chair using zippers, which had previously only been used for upholstered furniture. In contrast to the typical aesthetics of tubular steel furniture, which stresses the visual contrast of construction and cover material, Bellini opted here to completely envelope the supporting structure. The chair is thus lent a uniform appearance enhancing the quality of the natural leather. PR

88

Name:	**Queen Anne**
Designer:	**Robert Venturi**
Draft:	**1979-84**
Production:	**1984 to the present**
Manufacturer:	**Knoll International, Inc.,**
Measurements:	**H 98; W 68; D 61; seat height 49 cms**
Materials:	**molded multiplex, laminated plastic, imitation leather cushions**

Since the publication of his influential 1966 essay Complexity and Contradiction in Architecture, American architect Robert Venturi has been considered one of the founders of Postmodernism. He vividly described the principle underlying this style as "both-and" instead of "either-or," and brilliantly countered Mies van der Rohe's tenet of classic Modernity that "less is more" with "less is a bore".Venturi's most famous furniture design consists of a series of nine chairs, which he designed for Knoll International between 1979 and 1984.
By means of clichéd simplification, his chairs cite models from United States' and European furniture history, ranging from the eighteenth-century Queen Anne chair to Art Deco of the thirties. Venturi was interested in the image, the representative side, of these models. Thus, his two-piece structure for Queen

Anne is based on sawed-out and bent laminated wood panels for the back, legs, and seat which presents the chair as a silhouette copy, a backdrop. The Queen Anne chair shown here was presumably inspired by a Giles Grendey design dating from 1730 on display in the New York Metropolitan Museum. When seen from the side, the chair brings to mind the plywood furniture of Alvar Aalto or Marcel Breuer from the thirties; at the same time, the surfaces have been printed on both sides, revealing just how solid they are. The so-called "Grandmother" pattern on the surface, which Venturi also used to upholster one of his sofas, is similar to the laminates designed by the Milan Memphis group around the same time. In fact, the pattern consists of two motifs superimposed upon each other: a favorite tablecloth of the grandmother of colleague Robert Schwartz, and diagonal stripes, a quotation from paintings by artist Jasper Johns.

The numerous possibilities for the shapes and patterns in which the furniture is available result in complex, thoroughly contradictory statements. They are both an ironic commentary as well as an affirmation of the desire on the part of the consumer society to be linked into in a historic continuity. MSC

Tomorrow will be less.

Phillipe Starck, Designer, 1997

Sottsass
De Lucchi
Stiletto
Pesce
Branzi
Arad
Dubreuil
Morison
Gehry
Starck

9

1981-1990

Design as Lifestyle

Influenced by the economic upturn world-wide and major progress in the area of electronic data transmission, personal success and comfort of life become foregrounded as values, with the socio-political ideals of 1968 ceasing to be important. **Communications media** and **computers** conquer the private domain, which therefore becomes more significant and indeed, even starts to function as a place of work. Design becomes the expression of a personal **lifestyle**, a status symbol and a fashion. Following the committed, conceptual drafts of the 1970s, this leads to numerous new approaches interested less in fundamental problem solutions and more in an individual aesthetics. Alongside the numerous lone wolves, who are honored as the **stars** of the design scene, very few broad currents are to be discerned — at best passing trends can be seen.

The work of the **Memphis** designer group, founded in Milan in 1980, is the last successful attempt to establish an influential design concept; its protagonists include **Ettore Sottsass** and **Michele de Lucchi**. While Sottsass with his pop-like drafts had been an important figure in the world design scene as of the 1950s, Michele de Lucchi is a product of the radical design movement of the early 1970s. Memphis refers directly to the emerging **communications society** and represents the view that an object is only contemporary if it functions as a **medium**, that, like other media, also transports a message. The

practical quality of the object is thus less decisive than its meaning as a medium of expression. In this sense, the Memphis use naive, abstract shapes and a surface design composed of colorful and patterns laminates to provoke the onlooker. They take the stage as products of a media world which kitsch and art blend, and are an expression of the apolitical agenda of "**anything goes**".
The works of **Phillipe Starck**, one of the most stunning figures in international design, are less programmatic, but equally spectacular. Since Starck works unusually productively and successfully as an industrial designer in numerous areas, his original, elegantly curved drafts soon have an impact world-wide. They correspond to prevailing tastes — the mass public after all wants aesthetically appealing, but often also humorous designer objects.
Ron Arad, who lives in London, takes a different approach: he welds metal to create unique metal objects, thus emphasizing the artistic status of his objects. He is representative of a trend in which, quite independently of industrial production, glass, wicker, concrete or other unusual materials are processed to generate extravagant furniture. The variety of styles ranges from the expressive raw works of an Arad via **Stiletto's** objects reminiscent of ready-mades, to the **Neo-Baroque** of an André Dubreuil.
Jasper Morrison, an English designer, is consciously anonymous and restrained in his work: objects which stand out for formal consistency and their reduction to the necessary. Here, the return to a more pragmatic design is already discernible - which most recently has increasingly endeavored to enter into dialogue with industry.

89

Name:	**Seggiolina da Pranzo**
Designer:	**Ettore Sottsass**
Draft:	**1980**
Production:	**as of 1980**
Manufacturers:	**Studio Alchimia, Milan**
Measurements:	**H 84; W 37.5; D 47.5 cms**
Materials:	**pressboard, laminated plastic, chrome-plated steel**

Ever since the 1950s, Ettore Sottsass has been known for his provocative, pioneering designs. It is safe to say that he is largely responsible for Italy leading the way in the international design world. From 1976 to 1980, he worked for Alchimia, a group of designers that coalesced in Milan in 1976, and in 1980 he founded the influential Memphis group. During this time, he worked together with other Italian designers such as Alessandro Mendini, Andrea Branzi and Michele De Lucchi, to elaborate a design theory based on the new conditions created by the age of electronic mass media. In their view, the media alter human perception to such an extent that a design object today has to convey messages and emotions like any other means of communication. In addition, Sottsass' interest in Far Eastern philosophies is reflected in the often spiritual content of his designs.
The supernatural, magical aspect of a design object is also alluded to by the name of the group Alchimia. It suggests that the designer's art is to refine everyday banal objects and materials by releasing them from their typical

use and redefining them.
With this goal in mind, Sottsass turned to laminated plastic, which had been utilized since the 1950s to upgrade or protect wooden surfaces and, with its trivial decorations, had come to symbolize the petty bourgeois home. His designs for laminate patterns combine graphic or geometric structures with imitation wood or marble, African symbols, comic-strip motifs and aggressive colors. With the help of these laminates, which are actually sterile and lifeless, he transformed the surfaces of his objects into expressive media.
Sottsass designed the Seggiolina da Pranzo for "Alchimia" in 1980. The somewhat restrained colors and patterns support the central design element, the two grips on the back-rest. Freed from their original function, these grips, together with the sharp-edged cubes and the saccharine pastels of the laminate, blend to form one unit. This, in turn, triggers associations, such as kitchen, kitsch, food or ice cream parlor, which, by adding an artistic dimension to the chair, broaden the user's experience of it. MK

90

Name:	**First**
Designer:	**Michele De Lucchi**
Draft:	**1983**
Production:	**1983 to the present**
Manufacturer:	**Memphis s.r.l., Pregnana Milanese, Milan**
Measurements:	**H 90; W 66; D 46 cms; seat height 45,5 cms**
Materials:	**varnished tubular steel, varnished wood, rubber**

Michele De Lucchi was one of the cofounders of the Milan designer group Memphis, which emerged at the end of 1980 around the central figure of Ettore Sottsass. The group's very first exhibition unleashed a frenzy of enthusiasm. Since then, the shrill, sensual, and playful designs produced by Memphis have exploded all academic convention and substantially influenced the world of design.
G. S. Sowden, also a cofounder of Memphis, writes: "The ornamental style belongs to the world of electronics, just as functionalism is part of the world of machines and machine aesthetics." The prevalent criterion for design was no longer the ability to solve technical problems, but rather the object's capacity for communication. It was necessary to confront the multiplicity of Postmodern styles in order to capture the Zeitgeist in a fast-paced, experimental design idiom.
First by Michele de Lucchi was one of the few designs

intended for the broad public, and quickly became a bestseller. The back and armrest construction is a true eye-catcher. It consists of a steel tube, bent to form a circle, which supports a flexible backrest involving a round wooden disk on rubber bearings and two wooden spheres as armrests. The tube is welded to the front legs of the simple stool, which forms the seat frame, almost completely engulfing the sitter. Although the construction is extremely stable, the reduced elements radiate a strong impression of lightness. The restrained use of decorative elements gives First an almost classic air among the Memphis objects, making it suitable for furnishing conventional interiors. MK

91

Name:	**Consumer's Rest**
Designer:	**Stiletto**
Draft:	**1983**
Production:	**since 1984**
Manufacturer:	**Stiletto Studios, Berlin**
Measurements:	**H 94; W 73.5; D 76; seat height 45 cms**
Materials:	**varnished steel, plastic**

Like Marcel Duchamp's ready-mades, Consumer's Rest is an everyday object chosen from among vast numbers of manufactured goods, reinterpreted, and invested with a new function.
Stiletto, who refers to himself as a practitioner of design and has been involved in experimental graphic design and other forms of art since 1981, says of his furniture designs: "They are to have a lucid structure, fulfill their intended function in terms of length times width times height, be industrially sound, stable, and solid, serially produced. I can meet these conditions most easily when I use containers taken from the everyday consumer cycle as my starting material.... Redesign here has less to do with recycling and more with rebirth. The design is about soul and character, not 'packaging design'."
Stiletto is not concerned with improving a product; instead, he simply makes use of what is available and has stood the test of time. Department stores and supermarkets but also junk yards provide plenty of

ideas and material.
The point of departure here is a supermarket shopping cart, a standard, ubiquitous everyday object, which hardly appears to have "design value."
Stiletto takes the shopping cart apart, reshapes it, and sprays each half with different color tones. The transparent covers are made of the thick, soft foil normally used only for industrial purposes, for example in swinging doors in warehouses. They alone ensure that the seat, armrests, and back afford a minimum of comfort, and make clear that what we are looking at is indeed for sitting.
Consumer's Rest and a smaller children's version, Short Rest, have been manufactured by Brüder Siegel in Leipheim, Germany since 1990. PR

92

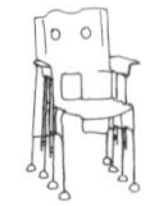

Name: **Greene Street**
Designer: **Gaetano Pesce**
Draft: **1984**
Production: **1986-1995**
Manufacturer: **Vitra AG, Basel**
Measurements: **H 94.5; W 65; D 55 cm**
Materials: **polyester resin, steel, polyurethane foam**

Gaetano Pesce, an Italian who lives in New York, is one of the most original contemporary architects and designers. Since the early 1970s, he has explored the technical and structural characteristics of moldable materials such as polyester resin, polyurethane foam, balls of material or felt. In his furniture designs, Pesce unites semi-industrial manufacturing processes with an individual, amorphous design. At the same time, Pesce animates the materials used by forging a link between their tactile and irrational aspects and human life and vulnerability. His designs repeatedly irritate the viewer familiar with sterile, interchangeable industrial objects, by confronting us with spontaneous, aleatory elements.
The chair Greene Street, named after the street in which Pesce's studio is located, is typical of many of his expressive objects. Like a many-legged insect, the chair rests on eight legs made of thin steel rods, which provide at best an unsteady base. The soft, hemispherical plastic units that function as feet bring to mind suction cups, while the continuations of the steel rods protrude like

bones out of the body of firm polyester resin. In the backrest (its unevenness is emphasized still further by a high-gloss varnish) we can discern a face, with eyes and mouth. A red, not yet varnished prototype also featured a "nose" formed by a slot in the plastic. The red varnish, which creates the expressive black-and-red contrast Pesce often deploys, is an unmistakable feature of each chair, for it is always applied at a different juncture.
A similar chair-leg construction to that used in Greene Street is to be found in the stool which Pesce developed as early as 1973. This precursor also exhibits another characteristic Pesce feature: an incompletely dyed plastic seat; it is shot through with different colors and seems to pin-point the process which created the chair. Here, too, each chair is an original, since new color variations were used for each production run. MK

93

Name:	**Animali Domestici**
Designer:	**Andrea Branzi**
Draft:	**1985**
Production:	**since 1985**
Manufacturer:	**Zabro s.r.l., Milan**
Measurements:	**H 95; W 60; D 65; seat height 45 cms**
Materials:	**varnished wood, wood**

Animali Domestici (pets) is a series of furniture and garments designed by Andrea Branzi and his wife, Nicoletta, in order to nurture the domestic sphere anew in keeping with future demands. According to Branzi, a large part of our life and work will take place at home. As the germ cell of social and urban life, the home is taking on ever greater importance, and new developments in telecommunications will help shape our notion of the world from within the home. Various individual and social cultures are thus drafting a new language which is multifaceted and ephemeral, yet common to us all, similar to the idiom that already exists in pop music.

Branzi terms the objects he has designed for the new culture of the private sphere Animali Domestici - for they are to be understood as pets, living beings from a foreign yet related world. As hybrids of archetypal materials and anonymous industrial goods, a combination of Arte Povera and precision design, they lend their very own expression to the search for possible ways to combine technical feasibility and respect for nature. MSC

94

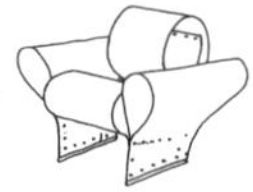

Name: Well Tempered Chair
Designer: Ron Arad
Draft: 1986
Production: 1986-1993
Manufacturer: Vitra AG, Basel
Measurements: H 80; W 98.5; D 80; seat height approx. 48 cms
Materials: high-grade sheet steel, thumb screws

In his seemingly surrealist furniture, Ron Arad favors materials and objects from areas outside the domain of traditional furniture production. Since the mid-eighties his London studio has increasingly produced individual pieces made of sheet steel, and he always mischievously exploits their formal and functional possibilities to the full. The sculptural forms often have an unexpected impact which first emerges during use, and are just as much a result of graphic design as the experimental work that goes on in the workshop. The sort of minimalist attitude expressed by the "Well Tempered Chair," designed for the "Vitra Edition," is quite a novelty in comparison to Arad's earlier works.
Here, Arad reduces the massive volume of the classic armchair, leaving only the pure surface of its rounded forms. At first glance, the cool gleam and the sharp-edged cut of the metal raise doubts whether the object can actually be used. But the "Well Tempered Chair" offers a unique kind of sitting comfort: sitting amidst

the steel loops, which after some time take on the body temperature of the user, you waver between coziness and uncertainty. MSC

95

Name:	**Spine**
Designer:	**André Dubreuil**
Draft:	**1986**
Production:	**1986**
Manufacturer:	**André Dubreuil, London**
Measurements:	**H 88.5; W 56; D 73 cms**
Materials:	**blackened soft steel**

Before André Dubreuil began creating furniture and other objects in a smithy in 1985, he had worked in various fields - among other things, he had been an antiques dealer and an interior designer. His designs are characterized primarily by imaginative, ornate forms. Dubreuil sees the Rococo as an important source of inspiration for his work as a designer. "Perhaps I am decadent, but I love the Rococo. It is sensuous, cheerful - and slightly crazy. Why should I deprive my optic nerve of such pleasure?"

The Spine chair, Dubreuil's most famous and best-selling design, is a refined, sculptural object with dazzling curved lines. Its form calls to mind Rocaille ornamentation, a primary Rococo design element found in the bent iron garden chairs that were so popular in the 19th century.

Like all of Dubreuil's objects, Spine was painstakingly made by hand in small numbers. MK

96

Name:	**Thinking Man's Chair**
Designer:	**Jasper Morrison**
Draft:	**1986**
Production:	**as of 1987**
Manufacturers:	**Cappellini s.p.a., Como, Italy**
Measurements:	**H 69; W 65; D 90.5 cms; seat height 36 cms**
Materials:	**tubular and flat steel, varnished**

In the contemporary design world, Jasper Morrison's work is an deliberately straightforward idiom that starkly contrasts with the garish stylistic experiments of the 1980s. Morrison's designs do not foreground the designer's individual signature, but instead appear to be anonymous, functional everyday objects, and it is difficult to imagine a time when they did not exist. Only at second glance, do they prove to possess a complexity and expressiveness that is achieved precisely by minimizing formal means. Morrison often presents his works in sparsely furnished interiors that define the relationship of the things to the user and the latter's environment.

In Thinking Man's Chair, Morrison reduces the spacious club chair to a structure made of tubular and flat steel. The flexibility of the flat steel affords the seat only a slight degree of springiness, while the surface, uniformly varnished either in the rusty red of rust-proofing or in gray, highlights the simplicity of the material used. The elegantly curved tubular steel section forms both the back legs and arm-rests, and, together with the flawless, drawn-out construction, lends the chair a dynamics that evokes the streamlined design of the 1930s. In the room installation entitled "Some New Items for the House, Part II", put on show in 1989 by the Vitra furniture company in Facsimile, a Milan gallery, Morrison exhibited "Thinking Man's Chair" as well as a drawing which illustrates how metal plates are used in the chair's arm-rests. In an ironic allusion to the attributes of a "thinking man", they serve as a platform for a wine glass, bottle of wine, or ashtray. MK

97

Name:	**Ply Chair**
Designer:	**Jasper Morrison**
Draft:	**1988**
Production:	**1989 to the present**
Manufacturer:	**Vitra AG, Basel**
Measurements:	**H 84.5; W 39,5; D 47; seat height 47.5 cms**
Materials:	**plywood, birch veneer**

The work of English designer Jasper Morrison is characterized by simplicity and clarity. His ideas are the very opposite of so-called Postmodern products which, with their daring combinations of patterns, colors, and materials, contributed to the downfall of Functionalism.
In the skeletal construction of the Ply Chair, formal complexity has been reduced to a minimum. Here, the designer as auteur steps out of the limelight, completely eclipsed by the object's functionality. Morrison uses his materials unpretentiously but with great precision. A wooden cross with edges that taper toward the middle is attached underneath the seat for support, but at the same time allows the seat to yield during use. This feature, together with the gently curved backrest, make the Ply Chair unexpectedly comfortable in comparison to many expensive wood chairs.
The backrest of the chair is either open or slat-paneled, with a gently arched plywood leaf. Formal

austerity and straightforward materials also characterize the Ply Table, which came out a year later. However, both table and chair are produced at relatively high cost in order to guarantee aesthetic perfection. MSC

98

Name:	**Rolf's Chair**
Designer:	**Frank O. Gehry**
Draft:	**1990**
Production:	**1990**
Manufacturers:	**Knoll-Gehry Workshop, Santa Monica, California**
Measurements:	**H 106.5; W 51; D 57 cms, seat height 44.5 cms**
Material:	**laminated, bent maple wood**

Frank O. Gehry has made a name for himself with his unconventional, dynamic architecture. Indeed, since the 1980s he has been considered one of the most important contemporary architects. In 1972, prior to his international breakthrough, he designed Easy Edges, a sensational cardboard furniture series. Experimental Edges, made of the same material, followed in 1982.

In a workshop set up by the Knoll furniture company, in 1989 Gehry began work on a new principle for developing furniture that could be serially produced. Inspired by the construction of wicker baskets, he wove elastic strips of laminated wood to create light-weight constructions, sometimes in voluminous forms with three-dimensional curves, in other cases with the laminated strips strictly parallel to one another. In the prototypes, Gehry riveted these strips; however, when the chair was serially produced they were glued in order to preserve the character of the weave. In addition to affording a comfortable cushioning effect, the strips reduced the weight of the chair and the amount of wood needed. This fit in well with Gehry's goal in designing the Bentwood Collection - to manufacture inexpensive, practical furniture for mass production.

The series distinctly stands out from bentwood furniture such as that designed by the Thonet brothers, Aalvar Aalto or Charles Eames, for the latter all opted for a separation of the constructive elements into back-rest, seat and weight-bearing frame. By contrast, thanks to his weaving technique, Gehry was able to fuse the elements into one single structure. An experimental chair design by the Gebr. Thonet company, formed from just two rods of bentwood, employs a similar approach in order to achieve a more straightforward construction, the same goal attained by forming a chair from just one sheet of laminated wood, a technique explored by numerous designers. A little-known 1939 design by Aalvar Aalto features a construction that is astonishingly similar to Rolf's Chair shown here.

Gehry dedicated Rolf's Chair, a variation on the serially produced model High Sticking Side Chair, to Swiss furniture entrepreneur Rolf Fehlbaum, for whose company Gehry designed the Vitra Design Museum in 1989 and the Vitra Center in Birsfelden, near Basel, in 1992. While Rolf's Chair is open in front, the cube shape of the "High Sticking" side chair is reinforced by the strips of the seat, which run from the front edge of the seat to the bottom end of the back-rest. The open front of Rolf's Chair affords more leg space and underscores the impression of lightness and transparency - because it provides a glimpse of the "exposed" interior of the chair. A strut positioned cross-wise lends additional stability to the high back-rest, balancing out tension and compression.

A comparison between the exposed and yet voluminous structures of the Bentwood Collection furniture and the massive bodies of Experimental Edges highlights the central theme of Gehry's architecture, also manifested in both Vitra buildings: he endeavors to play with volumes. In his compositions, volumes are interconnected, rendered dynamic, transcended, or set in motion. MK

99

Name:	**W.W. Stool**
Designer:	**Philippe Starck**
Draft:	**1990**
Production:	**1992 to the present**
Manufacturer:	**Vitra AG, Basel**
Measurements:	**H 97; W 56; D 53 cms**
Materials:	**varnished sand-cast aluminum**

Philippe Starck describes himself as an autodidact who, at the age of nineteen, had already founded his first company for inflatable furniture. In the media he is regarded as a star. He came to fame in the late seventies and early eighties with his interiors for nightclubs and cafes in Paris, especially Café Costes (1984), which became famous for the three-legged chair sold worldwide that bore its name.
Starck caught the eye in 1982, when then-president of France, François Mitterand, commissioned the newcomer to furnish his private chambers in the Elysée Palace.
Since the beginning of the eighties, Starck has successfully created designs for industrial production in various sectors. Among his preferences are aluminum and more or less long, streamlined "horns." This is no doubt a legacy of his father who, as an aircraft mechanic and inventor, worked with this material and these forms. However, Starck does not attempt to imitate aerodynamic profiles but instead reinterprets

them biomechanically. His ingenuity appears inexhaustible, his repertoire of forms infinite. He christens his creations with names from science fiction novels, for example the "Ubik" series by the Italian manufacturer Driade, from the novel of the same name by American author Philip K. Dick.

The stool, or more accurately the W.W. Stool standing aid, is part of an imaginative office ensemble which Starck sketched for film director Wim Wenders in 1990. A sculptural look dominates the surrealist appearance of this object. On the one hand, a "stool" is defined as a piece of seating furniture; on the other, it is defined as a sprout, which implies a possible source of inspiration. Thus, the sculptural surface of the seat and back has the effect of a germinating rhizome, with three roots growing into the floor, while the shoot winds its way upward. The branching of the front "root" serves as footrest.

The biomechanical element in Starck's design style can be compared to that of Luigi Colani and his "bio-design"; both designers are also active in a wide range of design fields. PD

100

Name:	**Louis 20**
Designer:	**Philippe Starck**
Draft:	**1991**
Production:	**1992 to the present**
Producer:	**Vitra AG, Basel**
Measurements:	**H 84.5; W 59; D 60; seat height 47 cms**
Materials:	**blown polypropylene; polished aluminium**

Philippe Starck is regarded as the French figurehead in the area of New Design in the eighties. He has achieved an international reputation and creates designs for leading companies worldwide.
Starck is fascinated by the efficiency of modern production methods which allow the manufacture of low-cost articles, and he sometimes even demands the right to codefine pricing.
Since the end of the eighties he has combined tubular steel with plastic. The Dr. Glob series of chairs, which he designed for the Italian manufacturer Kartell in 1988, involves an interplay of contrasts in material and shape. The continuous angular front legs and seat made of pastel-colored plastic developed by swaging are complemented by black- or silver-lacquered round back legs which rise up to a curved back section. The contrast in materials is also a main feature of the stackable "Louis 20" chair. Here, the voluminous hollow front legs, the seat with the characteristic Starck front curve, and the springy

back section are blown from a single piece of polypropylene. The frame of the back legs is sturdily joined with an oversized fixing plate to the hollow plastic body so that the chair can be tilted on its back legs without any damage. Its subtle color scheme combined with the brilliance of the polished aluminum make this chair just as popular in private as in public spaces, and it is also suitable for outdoors. It can be easily dismantled into recyclable elements in only a few seconds by loosening the screws on the armrests and the fixing plate of the back legs.
Starck ironically named the chair Louis 20, poking fun at the French royal tradition of distinguishing kings of the same name by numbering them from IV to XVIII, including Louis XIV, the "Sun King," and of identifying styles during their respective reigns the same way. PD

Biographies

Hugo Alvar Henrik Aalto
born 1898 Kuortane, Finland
died 1976 Helsinki, Finland
34, 42

1916-1921: studied architecture at the Helsinki Polytechnic; 1923-1927: architectural studio in Jyväskylä, Finland; 1927-1933: architectural studio in Turku, Finland; 1928: member of Congrès Internationaux d'Architecture Moderne (CIAM); 1928-1930: designed the office building for the Turun Sanomat newspaper in Turku; 1929: worked with Otto Korhonen in an experimental workshop for laminated wood in Turku; 1929-33: built and furnished the tuberculosis sanitarium in Paimio; 1933-1976: architectural studio in Helsinki; 1935: set up the Artek furniture company; patented the first self-supporting wooden chair frame; 1937: built the Finnish pavilion at the world's fair in Paris; 1938: solo exhibition at the MoMA in New York; 1939: designed the Finnish pavilion for the New York world's fair; 1946-1948: professor at Massachusetts Institute of Technology, Cambridge, Massachusetts; 1947-1949: built the MIT dormitory; 1953: designed the main building of the Helsinki Technical University; 1957: received a Royal Institute of British Architects gold medal; until 1976: extensive activity as architect.
Alvar Aalto's major architectural endeavors range from regional planning, to churches and public buildings, to single-family houses. He was a pioneer in research on forming laminated wood in architecture and furniture construction.

Eero Aarnio
born 1932 Helsinki, Finland
75

1954-1957: studied at and graduated from the College of Applied Art in Helsinki; 1961: drafted rattan furniture for the firm Asko; 1962: founded his own design bureau; 1965: 1st prize in a famous Scandinavian competition for park and street furniture; 1964: participated in the Milan Triennial; 1969: distinction from the

American Institute of Interior Architects for the armchair Pastilli; 1991: participated in the exhibition "Masters of Modern Design" in the IBM Gallery, New York.

Jacques André
born 1904 Nancy, France
died 1985
43

Studied architecture; founded an architectural studio together with his brother Michel André; 1934: member of the Union des Artistes Modernes (UAM); starting in 1945: urban planning for the reconstruction of Saint-Dié, France; contact with Le Corbusier; industrial and public building projects; 1966: designed the Steel Museum in Jarville, France; 1972: built the Centre Tripostal, Nancy.
Architect Jacques André was concerned primarily with public buildings and industrial plants.

Ron Arad
born 1951 Tel Aviv, Israel
94

1971-1973: studied at the Art Academy in Jerusalem; 1973: moved to London; 1974-79: studied at the Architectural Association, London; 1979-81: worked in a London architectural studio; 1981: together with Caroline Thorman opened his own design studio, One Off Ltd. in London; first successful furniture designs; 1983: opened 'One Off' showroom in London; 1984: solo exhibition at Galerie Zeus, Milan; 1986: participated in the exhibition "Wohnen von Sinnen" at the Dusseldorf Museum of Art; 1989: established the design and architectural studio Ron Arad Associates, Ltd.; furniture designs for Vitra and Poltronova; 1990: together with Alison Brooks designs interior of the Tel Aviv opera house; participated in various exhibition, e.g., at Centre Georges Pompidou, Paris, and the Victoria and Albert Museum, London; designed the Soft Volumes furniture series for Moroso; solo exhibition "Sticks and Stones" at the Vitra

Design Museum, which also tours Tel Aviv, Darmstadt, and Warzaw; 1993: teaching activities at the College of Applied Art in Vienna; numerous designs for furniture companies; interior furnishings; 1994: established Ron Arad Associates branch office in Italy; exhibition "L'Esprit du Nomade" at the Fondation Cartier, Paris; designed a furniture series using laminated wood for Driade; 1995: solo exhibition at the Museum of Applied Art, Helsinki.
Ron Arad manufactures one-of-a-kind furniture pieces in his welding workshop. He also designs furniture for serial production and works as an interior designer.

Archizoom Associati
(**Andrea Branzi, Gilberto Coretti,**
Paolo Deganello, Massimo Morozzi;
and as of 1968:
Dario Bartolini, Lucia Bartolini)
78

1966: foundation of the architecture and design group Archizoom Associati; designed the exhibition "Superarchitettura" in Pistoia, and 1967 in Modena, Italy; 1968: created the Center of Eclectic Conspiracy for the Milan Triennial; 1969-1971: project "Non-Stop City"; 1972: participated in the exhibition "Italy: The New Domestic Landscape"; 1973: together with other architects the group established the Global Tools group.
Archizoom Associati drew on influences of Pop Art to formulate provocative, avant-garde ideas for reorganizing living space.

Grupo Austral
(Antoni Bonet, Jorge Ferrari Hardoy,
Juan Kurchan)
45

1937: Jorge Ferrari Hardoy received a degree in architecture from the University of Buenos Aires; subsequently traveled to Europe and worked in Le Corbusier's studio; 1939: established the architectural studio Grupo Austral in Buenos Aires; active in urban development and public building construction; 1944: developmental planning for San Juan, a city destroyed by an earthquake.

Mario Bellini
born 1935 Milan, Italy
87

Prior to 1959: received a doctorate in architecture from the Milan Polytechnic; 1961-1963: head of design at the La Rinascente department store chain; 1962: wins the Milan Triennial Compasso d'oro, the first of seven such distinctions; 1962-1965: professor at the College of Industrial Design, Venice; 1963: established an architectural studio together with Marco Romano; 1963: design consultant for Olivetti; developed a series of important typewriters and calculators for Olivetti; set up the environmental research group Environmedia; 1973: opened the design and architectural studio Studio Bellini in Milan; 1978: research and design consultant at Renault; as of 1979: member of the scholarly advisory council of the Milan Triennial; 1981: launched the magazine Album; 1982-1983: taught at the Applied Art College in Vienna; 1983-85: taught at the Domus Academy in Milan; as of 1986: editor-in-chief of the magazine Domus; numerous architectural projects worldwide; 1987: solo exhibition at the New York MoMA.
Mario Bellini is renowned worldwide as an architect, industrial designer, furniture designer, journalist, and lecturer.

Giandomenico Belotti
born 1922, Bergamo
71

as of 1938: trained as a sculptor under Mario Marini; studied at the Brera Art Academy in Milan; studied at Milan Polytechnic; doctorate at Venice University; requested by American Insituite of Architects to participate in R.S. Memorial Award; 1979: began working with Alias.
Belotti works in Milan as an internatioonally successful architect and

city planner.

Harry Bertoia
born 1915 San Lorenzo, Italy
died 1978 Bally, Pennsylvania
56

1930: emigrated to the United States; until 1936: studied at the Cass Technical College in Detroit; active in jewelry design and painting; 1937-1943: received a scholarship to the Cranbrook Academy of Art, Michigan, where he founded and directed the metal workshop; 1943: moved to California along with Charles and Ray Eames; assisted with their experiments in molding laminated wood for leg splints and aircraft components; designed acoustic sculptures made of wire; 1950: returned to Pennsylvania on invitation from Knoll; designed a series of wire chairs for Knoll; wire sculptures for the Massachusetts Institute of Technology chapel; 1953: consultant for Knoll, otherwise active only as a sculptor; 1956: received the American Institute of Architects' Craftsmanship Medal; further distinctions and lecturing positions.
Harry Bertoia saw himself first and foremost as a sculptor, although he brought his metalworking expertise to bear on areas of the applied arts.

André Bloc
born 1896 Algiers, Algeria
died 1966 New Delhi, India
53

1898: emigrated to France; until 1920: trained as an engineer; in 1920: worked in a motor factory, subsequently in a turbine factory; 1921: met Le Corbusier; 1922: organizational head of the magazine Science et Industrie; 1923: organizational head of Revue de l'Ingénieur magazine; 1924: established the Revue Générale du Caoutchouc journal; 1930: founded the magazine L'Architecture d'Aujourd'hui; as of 1940: first sculpture projects; 1949: set up Art d'Aujourd'hui magazine; 1949 and 1956: large-scale sculptures in Paris; early fifties: established the group Espaces; 1952: designed the Bellevue house in Meudon; until 1966: worked predominantly as a sculptor and interior designer; various projects in Tehran, Nice, Jacksonville, Dakar.

Andrea Branzi
born 1938 Florence, Italy
93

Prior to 1966: studied architecture in Florence; 1966: cofounder of the group Archizoom; 1969-1971: involved in the Archizoom "Non-Stop City" project; 1971-1973: several articles for the magazine Casabella; 1973: dissolution of Archizoom; worked as an exhibit designer for the Milan Triennial and as a freelance designer; 1977: cofounded the Studio Alchimia design group; 1980: anthology of his theoretical writings appears entitled Moderno, postmoderno, millenario; 1982: worked together with the Memphis group; director of the Domus Academy; 1983-1984: instructor at the University of Palermo; 1983-1987: publisher of the magazine Modo; 1984: published "La Casa Calda"; as of 1984: guest lecturer at universities in France, the United States, Japan, Argentina, Brazil, Canada; 1986: published "Animali Domestici"; 1987: received the Compasso d'Oro special prize for his oeuvre; as of 1991: director of the Domus Design Agency in Tokyo; 1991-1993: participated in the "Citizen Office" project for the Vitra Design Museum; 1992: published Luoghi, an anthology of his most important projects from 1966-1991.
Andrea Branzi is one of the leading Italian design theorists.

Marcel Breuer
born 1902 Pécs, Hungary
died 1981 New York, New York
21, 26, 31, 36

1920-1924: studied at the Vienna Academy of the Arts, and at the Bauhaus in Weimar; 1924: worked in an architectural studio in Paris;

1925: head of the Bauhaus furniture workshop; designed the B 3 tubular steel club chair; 1925: numerous additional tubular steel furniture designs; 1926: together with Kalman Lengyel set up the Standard Möbel company; 1927: furnished the Piscator residence in Berlin; 1928: opened his own architectural studio in Berlin together with Walter Gropius; 1930: participated in the exhibition of the Société des Artistes Décoratifs in Paris; 1932-1934: spent time in Switzerland and Budapest; 1932: collaborated with the Swiss company Embru; 1934: designed the Doldertal houses in Zurich for Sigfried Giedion; 1935: emigrated to England; opened his own architectural studio in London together with architect F. R. S. Yorke; developed laminated wood furniture for Isokon; 1937: moved to the United States; taught at Harvard University; 1937-1941: launched an architectural studio in Cambridge, Massachusetts, with Walter Gropius; 1941: started his own architectural studio; 1946: transferred his office to New York; built numerous private houses; 1947: built his own residence in New Canaan, Connecticut; 1948: solo exhibition at the MoMA, New York; 1956: head of Marcel Breuer & Associates; took part in designing the UNESCO buildings in Paris.
Along with Mies van der Rohe, Marcel Breuer was the most influential Bauhaus furniture designer and left behind an important legacy of architectural work.

Achille Castiglioni
born 1918 Milan, Italy
60, 79

Prior to 1944: architectural degree from Milan Polytechnic; 1944: together with his brothers Livio and Pier Giacomo opened an architectural studio; worked with Livio until 1952, and with Pier Giacomo until 1968; focused mainly on urban planning, construction projects, and industrial design; 1952: worked with Pier Giacomo Castiglioni as an interior and exhibition designer; 1956: cofounder of Associazione per il Disegno Industriale (ADI); designed the exhibition "Colori e forme nella casa d'oggi" in Villa Olmo, Como; 1962: designed the Gavina branch office in Milan; 1963: designed the exhi-

bition "Vie d'acqua da Milano al mare" in the Palazzo Reale, Milan; 1969: received a doctoral degree; 1969-1977: taught architecture at the Turin Polytechnic; 1977-1980: professor of interior design at Turin Polytechnic; 1981: professor of interior design at Milan Polytechnic; 1984: traveling exhibition "Achille Castiglioni" in Vienna, Berlin, and Milan; 1986: honorary member of the association of industrial designers at the Royal Academy of Art, London; recipient of seven Compasso d'Oro awards.
Achille Castiglioni is a pioneer in innovative industrial design in Italy.

Pier Giacomo Castiglioni
born 1913 Milan, Italy
died 1968 Milan, Italy
60

Prior to 1938: completed studies in architecture at Milan Polytechnic; 1938: designed the Phonola radio; specialized in lighting systems as well as furniture design and technical instruments; 1944: together with Achille and Livio Castiglioni opened an architectural studio; 1952: Livio Castiglioni left the group; until 1968: cooperated with Achille Castiglioni in design interiors and exhibitions.

Luigi (Lutz) Colani
born 1928 Berlin, Germany
82

1946: studied painting and sculpture at the Berlin College of Visual Arts; 1948: studied aerodynamics in Paris; carried out futuristic studies for car and motorcycle magazines; 1952-1953: high-speed and material research for the Douglas aircraft company in California; 1954: returned to Europe; received the Goldene Rose award for a Fiat car-body; worked for Alfa-Romeo, Lancia, VW, and BMW; 1972: experimental design for Thyssen, Boeing, Rosenthal, Rockwell (NASA), Villeroy & Boch; 1973: established a Colani Design Center in Japan; 1983: moved to Japan; 1988: professor emeritus at the University of Bremen; 1990: architectural projects in Japan and Thailand; 1992: first extensive Colani retrospective in Dortmund; previous exhibitions in Japan and Switzerland; 1993: designed computer hardware for VOBIS; 1995: opened a Colani Design Center in Lünen. Colani's designs, which ranged from airplanes to furnishings and tableware, have helped popularize organic design.

Joe Colombo
born 1930 Milan, Italy
died 1971 Milan
73

Until 1949: studied art at the Brera Academy, Milan; 1950-1954: studied architecture at the Polytechnic of Milan; worked as a painter; 1952: member of the Nucleare movement led by Enrico Baj and Sergio Dangelo; 1954: worked together with Bruno Munari, Enzo Mari and Gillo Dorfles within the framework of the Mac-Spazio-Movement; drafted three open-air rest areas with television installations for the X Milan Triennial; 1956: realization of first architectural draft; 1959-1962: worked for his family's electrical firm; his first investigation into industrial design; 1962: founded his own bureau of architecture and design in Milan; 1964: IN-Arch prize for the interior furnishing of a hotel on Sardinia; one gold and two silver medals from the Milan Triennial; 1969: designed an interior for the exhibition "Visiona 1", Cologne; participated in the exhibition "Qu'est-ce que le design?", Musée des Arts Décoratifs, Paris.
In his brief creative period Joe Colombo became one of the most important and popular industrial designers. He united a radically innovative approach with a plastic, artistically shaped idea of form.

Hans Coray
born 1906 Wald, Switzerland
died 1991
44

Prior to 1929: studied Romance languages; 1931: middle-school teacher in Aarau and Zuoz; first furniture designs; 1932-8: continued education in graphology, astrology, religious philosophy, and design; began work in metal design; 1941: participated in a course on metalworking in Zurich; as of 1945: active as a designer, artist, and art dealer; 1983: solo exhibition at the Strauhof building in Zurich.

Michele De Lucchi
born 1951 Ferrara, Italy
90

1969-1975: studied architecture in Ferrara and at the Florence Art College; 1973: established the Cavart group; 1976/1977: assistant in the Department of Architecture at the University of Florence; 1976: set up the Architetture e altri Piaceri studio in Florence; 1977: moved to Milan; 1979: design consultant for Olivetti; 1980: participated in the group Studio Alchimia; 1981: cofounder of Memphis; 1983: presented a prefabricated house at the Milan Triennial; 1986: established Solid, a group of young designers in Milan; along with Giancarlo Fassina designed the Tolomeo lamp; 1986: instructor at the Domus Academy in Milan; designed office and apartment buildings; 1987: taught at the Cranbrook Academy of Art, Michigan; 1991: won the competition to redesign the Deutsche Bank branch offices; 1991-1993: participated in the "Citizen Office" project for the Vitra Design Museum.
Until the eighties, Michele De Lucchi was involved in experiments in the area of New Design; today, he is one of Italy's most successful architects, theorists, and industrial designers.

André Dubreuil
born 1951 Lyon, France
95

As of 1969: studied at the Inchbald School of Design, London; 1973-1976: worked as a freelance interior designer, subsequently as an antique dealer; 1983: experiments with Trompe l'oeuil effects; as of 1985: furniture drafts, exhibitions in London, Paris, Tokyo, New York.

Charles Eames
born 1907 Saint Louis, Missouri
died 1978 Saint Louis, Missouri
46, 48, 50, 52, 64, 67

1925-1928: studied architecture at Washington University; 1928-1930: worked in various architectural studios; 1930: opened his own architecture studio together with Charles M. Gray, and later with Walter E. Pauley; 1935: established a new architectural studio with Robert T. Walsh; planning for the St. Mary Church in Helena, Arkansas; 1937: first contact with Eero Saarinen; 1938: received a scholarship to the Cranbrook Academy of Art in Michigan through Eliel Saarinen; 1939: taught design at the Cranbrook Academy of Art; 1940: together with Eero Saarinen won first prize in the MoMA "Organic Design in Home Furnishings" competition; head of the Department of Industrial Design at the Cranbrook Academy of Art; 1941: married Ray Kaiser.

Ray Eames, née Kaiser
born 1912 Sacramento, California
died 1988 Saint Louis, Missouri
48, 50, 52, 64, 67

Prior to 1933: studied painting at the May Friend Bennet School in Millbrook, New York; until 1937: took courses in portrait painting at the Hofman School; 1937: participated in the first exhibition of American abstract artists at the Riverside Museum in New York; 1940: matriculated at the Cranbrook Academy of Art; 1941: married Charles Eames.

Charles and Ray Eames

1941-1943: designed stretchers and leg splints from molded laminated wood which they produced with the help of the Evans company in Los Angeles; 1946: exhibition of experiments in molded laminated wood at the Museum of Modern Art in New

York; Eames furniture designs were manufactured by Herman Miller; 1948: participated in "Low-Cost Furniture Design," a MoMA competition; 1949: built the Case Study House No. 8; starting around 1955: extensive activities as photographers and filmmakers; 1964: honorary degrees from the Pratt Institute in New York; 1964-1965: IBM pavilion at the New York world's fair; 1969: participated in the exhibition at the Musée des Art Décoratifs in Paris, "Qu'est-ce que le design?"; 1970-1971: Eliot Norton Chair of Poetry at Harvard University; 1973: exhibition at the Museum of Modern Art in New York, "Furniture by Charles Eames."
Charles and Ray Eames worked primarily in the fields of architecture, furniture design, photography, film, exhibition design, and graphic design, and were trendsetters in international design as of 1945.

Frank Owen Gehry
born 1929 Toronto, Canada
81, 98

1947: moved from Toronto to Los Angeles; prior to 1954: studied architecture at the University of Southern California in Los Angeles; 1956-1957: studied urban planning at the Harvard Graduate School of Design; subsequently worked in the architectural studios of Viktor Gruen and Pereira & Luckman in Los Angeles, and at André Remondet in Paris; 1962: set up the Frank O. Gehry & Associates architectural studio in Los Angeles; 1969-1972: designed the block furniture series "Easy Edges"; 1974: taught at Yale University; was elected member of the American Institute of Architects; 1976: designed the Jung Institute in Los Angeles; 1978: built his own house in Santa Monica, California, as well as several other single-family residences; 1982-4: designed the Californian Aerospace Museum, Los Angeles; taught at Harvard University; 1983: received the Arnold W. Brunner Award from the American Academy of Arts and Letters; 1984: designed the Norton apartment house in Venice, California; 1987: exhibition entitled "The Architecture of Frank O. Gehry" at the Walker Art Center in Minneapolis; 1989: built the Vitra Design Museum in Weil am Rhein as well as the Schnabel residence in Los

Angeles; received the Pritzker architecture prize from the Hyatt Foundation; 1992: won the Japanese Praemium Imperiale from the Japanese Art Association; 1993: designed the American Center in Paris; 1994: built the Birsfelden Vitra Center near Basel, Switzerland. Frank O. Gehry is one of the most important contemporary American architects.

Willy Guhl
born 1915 Stein am Rhein, Switzerland
59

1930-1933: trained in cabinetmaking in Schaffhausen; 1939: opened his own workshop; 1946/47: began working with reclining chairs; designed the first plastic-shell chair in Europe; 1948: participated in the MoMA competition "Low-Cost Furniture Design"; 1951-1980: head of interior design at the Vocational Arts College in Zurich; 1954: designed a garden chair and other products for the Eternit AG company; 1965-1980: head of product design at the Vocational Arts College in Zurich.
Trained as a craftsman, Willy Guhl became one the most influential industrial designers in Switzerland.

René Herbst
born 1891, Paris, France
died 1982, Paris, France
30

1908-14: studied architecture in Paris and took various vocational courses in London and Frankfurt; 1921: first exhibition at the Salon of the Société des Artistes Décorateurs; 1925: Member of the jury for Société des Artistes Décorateurs; 1930: cofounder of Union des Artistes Modernes (UAM); 1935: along with Le Corbusier, Fernand Léger, and others participated in the Exposition International de Bruxelles; 1946, 1949, and 1955: president of the Union des Artistes Modernes; 1950-1969: president of the Form Utiles group; 1951: published a text about Jean Puiforcat; 1954: published a text about

Pierre Chareau; 1954, 1957, and 1960: architect for the Xth, XIth and XIIth Milan Triennials.
René Herbst worked as an architect, interior designer, exhibition designer, and furniture designer.

Josef Hoffmann
1870 Pirnitz, Moravia
died 1956 Vienna, Austria
12, 13, 14

Prior to 1892: studied architecture at the State Academy of Arts and Crafts in Brno; 1892-1895: continued studies at the Academy of Visual Arts in Vienna, as well as in Munich; 1895: established the Siebener Club, whose members also included Josef Maria Olbrich and Koloman Moser; study-related travels to Southern Italy; 1896-1899: staff member in the Otto Wagner architectural studio; 1897: joined the Viennese Secession; 1899-1836: professor of architecture, interior design, and enamel painting at the Viennese Academy of Applied Art; 1900: designed the hall for the Viennese Secession at the Paris world's fair; 1902: traveled to England with Koloman Moser; was introduced to Charles Rennie Mackintosh; 1903: established the Wiener Werkstätte; 1905: built and furnished a sanitarium in Purkersdorf near Vienna as well as Palais Stoclet in Brussels; 1908: cofounder of the Österreichischer Werkbund; 1920: chief architect for the city of Vienna; 1925: designed the Austrian pavilion at the Exposition des Arts Décoratifs, Paris; 1932: created terrace houses for the International Werkbund housing estate.
Josef Hoffmann's work as an architect, furniture designer, and craftsman underwent numerous trends and styles and influenced both Classic Modernism and Postmodernism.

Vlastislav Hofman
born 1884 Jicin, Czechoslovakia
died 1964 Prague
17

1902-1907: studied at the Czechoslovak University under Professors J. Fanta, J.E. Koula and J. Schulz; worked in the planning department of the Prague municipal authorities; member of the co-operative Artel and of the artists' association Mánes; 1911: left the artists' association Mánes, joined the group Skupina vytvarnich umelco (group of artists); journalistic activities for the magazines Volne smery (Clear Paths) and Umelecky mesicnik (monthly art magazine); 1912: returned to the Mánes group; 1913: participated in the competition for erecting the Zizka monument on the Vitkov hill in Prague; 1918: participated in the first exhibition of the Tvrdosijni (The Stubborn Ones) group; 1925: gold medal from the Exposition Internationale des Arts Décoratifs et Industriels in Paris; 1937: Grand Prix at the art and technology exhibition in Paris; 1940: Grand Prix at the Milan Triennial.
Hofman worked as an architect, designer, painter and set-designer and was a protagonist of the Czechian modern age.

Arne Jacobsen
born 1902 Copenhagen, Denmark
died 1971 Copenhagen, Denmark
61

Trained in masonry; 1924: completed studies at the Copenhagen Technical College; 1925: won a silver medal at the Paris world's fair for a chair design; until 1927: studied architecture at the Royal Art Academy in Copenhagen; 1927-1930: worked in the Paul Holsoe architectural studio; 1929: presented the circular house of the future in an exhibition at the Royal Art Academy in Copenhagen; 1930-1971: runs his own architectural studio; extensive work as an architect; 1930-1935: designed an apartment complex in Bellevue, the Copenhagen beach district; 1937-1942: designed the City Hall in

Arhus; 1945-1947: emigrated to Sweden; 1956-1965: professor at the Royal Art Academy in Copenhagen; 1958-1960: designed and furnished the Royal Hotel in Copenhagen; 1957: received a silver medal at the Milan Triennial; 1962: member of the American Institute of Architects; 1966: honorary doctorate from Oxford University; 1967: designed the Cylinda Line product series for the Danish company Stelton; 1971: received a gold medal from the Frankfurt Architecture Academy; 1961-1971: designed the Danish National Bank, Copenhagen (completed in 1978).
Arne Jacobsen was one of the most important Scandinavian architects and industrial designers.

Pierre Jeanneret
born 1896 Geneva, Switzerland
died 1967
27, 28, 29

1913-1915 and 1918-1921: studied architecture at the École des Beaux Arts, Geneva; 1921-1923: worked with the Perret brothers in their studio; 1923-1940: worked together with his cousin Le Corbusier, and with Charlotte Perriand as of 1927; 1926-1927: with Le Corbusier won first prize for the competition to design the League of Nations Palace in Geneva; 1945: occasionally worked with Jean Prouvé; 1951-1965: director of the Architecture School of Chandigarh in India.

Gerd Lange
born 1931, Wuppertal
83

1956: completed studies at the Arts and Crafts School (now College of Design) in Offenbach; 1961: founded his own design studio in Kapsweyer; 1965: drafted the Farmer furniture series; 1979: first prize in the competition on seating for the Alte Oper opera house in Frankfurt; numerous drafts as an industrial designer for Drabert, de Sede, Wogg AG, Steelcase Strafor and others.

Le Corbusier
(Charles-Edouard Jeanneret-Gris)
born 1887 La Chaux-de-Fonds, Switzerland
died 1965 Cap Martin, France
27, 28, 29

1900: trained as an engraver at the La Chaux-de-Fonds Vocational Arts College; 1905: designed Villa Fallet (his first building project); 1908: worked in Auguste Perret's architectural studio in Paris; 1910-1911: lived in Germany; apprentice of Peter Behrens; 1912-1914: taught architecture at the La Chaux-de-Fonds Vocational Arts College; 1914: designed the Domino house; 1917: resettled in Paris; also active as a painter; 1918: together with painter A. Ozenfant published the programmatic treatise "Après le Cubisme"; 1920: launched the journal L'Esprit nouveau; took on the pseudonym "Le Corbusier"; 1922: built the Ozenfant residence; 1923: published "Vers une nouvelle architecture"; 1925: designed the Pavillon de l'Esprit Nouveau at the Exposition des Arts Décoratifs, Paris; designed a housing estate in Bordeaux-Pessac; 1927: designed experimental houses for the Weissenhof Settlement in Stuttgart; 1928: cofounder of the Congrès Internationaux d'Architecture Moderne (CIAM); 1929: cooperated with Charlotte Perriand and Pierre Jeanneret on furniture designs; 1942-1944: developed the Modulor system of proportions; 1944: published Charta of Athens; 1950-1954: built the church Notre-Dame-du-Haut in Ronchamp; until 1969: numerous architectural projects and publications.
As an architect and theorist, Le Corbusier was responsible for promoting a reduced form of Modernist architecture and is considered one of the most influential twentieth-century architects.

Adolf Loos
born 1870 Brno, Czech Republic
died Kalksburg, Austria
8

Studied in Liberec, subsequently at the Technical College of Dresden; 1893-1895: stay in the United States; worked in the bureau of architect Louis H. Sullivan; 1897: returned to Vienna, worked in the bureau of architect Carl Mayreder; journalistic activities; 1899: realization of first work with the interior furnishing of the Viennese Café Museum, dining room furnishing of the Stössler apartment, Vienna; furnishing of the business premises of the tailors Goldmann & Salatsch, Vienna; as of 1899: further activities as an interior designer, primarily in office and apartment furnishings; 1908: published the article "Ornament and Crime"; 1909-1911: construction of the business premises of the tailors Goldmann & Salatsch in Vienna; 1910: began working in house building; 1912: founded a building school; 1920-1922: senior architect at the Viennese housing scheme department; 1922: moved to Paris; drafts for Tristan Tzara and Josephine Baker among others; 1928: returned to Vienna.

Hans Luckhardt
born 1890 Berlin
died 1954 Bad Wiessee, Germany
and
Wassili Luckhardt
born 1889 Berlin
died 1972 Berlin
35, 41

Hans Luckhardt studied at the Technical University in Karlsruhe, Wassili Luckhardt at the Technical University in Dresden and in Charlottenburg, near Berlin; 1921: the Luckhardt brothers start working together; 1922-1923: first building project: residence in Berlin's West End; 1924: began working with Alfons Anker; 1927: first experiments with chairs containing moving parts; first tubular

steel furniture; 1928: several building projects; model home at the "Heim und Technik" exhibition in Munich; 1930: published On the New Way of Life; 1952: Hans Luckhardt is made professor at the Berlin College for Visual Arts; 1956: Wassili Luckhardt becomes a member of the Berlin Academy of the Arts; Lichtarchitektur published by Wassili Luckhardt and Walter Köhler; 1957: Bavarian State Public Utilities Building in Munich designed by Wassili Luckhardt; received the Art Prize of the City of Berlin.
The creative work of Hans and Wassili Luckhardt had a great influence on architecture in postwar Germany.

Charles Rennie Mackintosh
born 1868 Glasgow
died 1928 London
9

1884: worked in the office of architect John Hutchinson; as of 1885: night school courses at the Glasgow School of Art; as of 1889: worked as a draughtsman in the architect's office J. Honeyman & Keppie; 1890: study trip to France and Italy with the aid of a grant; 1890: founded the group The Four together with Margaret Macdonald (as of 1900 Mackintosh's wife), Frances Macdonald and Herbert MacNair; 1897: won the competition for the extension of the Glasgow School of Art; 1900: presented several furniture drafts at the annual exhibition of the Viennese secession; 1901: second prize in the competition "House of an Art Enthusiast" by the publisher A. Koch from Darmstadt for an interior décor; 1909: completed the extension building at the Glasgow School of Art; 1913: moved to London; further furniture and textile drafts as well as interior decoration; 1920; moved to Port-Vendres, France, numerous watercolour paintings.
Mackintosh played an important role in the development of Art Nouveau to the more rationalistic form of the classical modern age.

Enzo Mari
born 1932 Novara, Italy
85

1952-1956: studied literature and ancient philology at the Brera Art Academy in Milan; active in the psychology of perception; 1957: first design draft for the firm of Danese; since then has worked as a designer and adviser for Danese; as of 1963: coordination of the group of Italian artists Nuove Tendenze; 1965: organized the exhibition of Nuove Tendenze at the Biennial Zagreb; 1970: published "Funzione della ricerca estetica"; 1971: participated in the exhibition "Italy: The New Domestic Landscape" in the Museum of Modern Art, New York; 1976-1979: president of the Assoziazione per il Disegno Industriale; teaching assignments at Milan Polytechnical College, at the Centro Studi e Archivi della Communicazione in Parma, at the Art Academy of Carrara and at the Scuola Umanitaria in Milan; numerous international prizes and distinctions:
In Mari's creations as a designer, artist and graphic designer, aspects of social-theory and perception-psychology play an important role.

Mathieu Matégot
born 1910 Tapio-Sully, Hungary
54

Studied art in Budapest; 1931: moved to France; worked as a set-designer and architect; 1945: French citizenship; opened a furniture studio in Paris; 1949: member of the SAD (Société des Artistes Décorateurs); 1953: Grand Prix d'Honneur from the international exhibition in Madrid; 1954: interior design of the Tit Melin airport in Marocco and of the restaurant "La Saladière" in Paris; 1955: gold medal from the Société d'encouragement à l'art et l'industrie, Paris; 1959: stopped working as a furniture designer; worked primarily as a carpet designer; 1960: Compasso d'Oro from the XII. Triennial Milan; 1961-1965: professorship at the Academy of Art and Architecture in Nancy; until 1990: numerous works and exhibitions as a carpet designer; 1990: founded the Fondation Mathieu Matégot for carpet design in Bethesda, Maryland (USA).

Alessandro Mendini
born 1931 Milan, Italy
84

Studied architecture at Milan Polytechnic; prior to 1970: worked in the Nizzoli Associati architectural studio; 1970: member of the scholarly advisory council at the Domus Academy; 1970-1976; chief editor of the magazine Casabella; 1973: cofounder of the group Global Tools; 1977: cofounder of the Alchimia group; 1977-81: founder and chief editor of the magazine Modo; 1978: published Paesaggio Casalingo; received the Milan Triennial Compasso d'Oro; first "redesigns"; 1980: exhibition "L'oggetto banal banale" with Alchimia at the Venice Biennial; 1980-1985: chief editor of Domus magazine; 1981: published Architettura Addio; 1983: taught design at the Academy of Applied Art, Vienna; published Il progetto infelice; 1983: created designs for Alessi; 1983-1988: together with Achille Castiglioni and Aldo Rossi built the Casa della Felicità for Alessi; 1988-1994: built and furnished the Groninger Museum; 1993: solo exhibition at Artiscope, Brussels; 1994: designed numerous Swatch branch offices.
With his theoretical and practical work, and in particular his reinterpretations of designs by others, Alessandro Mendini has since the seventies made an important contribution to the Postmodern design discussion.

Ludwig Mies van der Rohe
born 1886 Aachen, Germany
died 1969 Chicago, Illinois
23, 32, 33

1897-1900: attended the Dombau College in Aachen, subsequently drafted stucco ornamentation for an interior decorator in Aachen; 1901-1907: studied with Bruno Paul and at the Berlin Vocational Arts College; 1907: first building designs; 1908-1911: worked together with architect Peter Behrens and Walter Gropius; subsequently as a freelance architect in Berlin; 1920: designed villas as well as exhibi-

tion architecture; 1926-1932: vice-president of the Deutscher Werkbund; 1927: general director of the Weissenhof Settlement, Stuttgart; designed and patented the first cantilever-base tubular steel chair; 1929: designed the German pavilion for the Barcelona world's fair as well as the metal furniture for both buildings; 1930: Villa Tugendhat in Brno, Czechoslovakia; replaced Hannes Meyer as Bauhaus director; 1931: signed a contract with Thonet for the exclusive marketing of fifteen chair designs; 1938: emigrated to the United States; professor in the Department of Architecture at the Armour Institute (later the Illinois Institute of Technology), Chicago; at the same time ran his own studio in Chicago; 1940: designed a number of the buildings at the Armour Institute; 1958: designed the Seagram Building, New York; 1962-1967: designed the New National Gallery in Berlin.
Ludwig Mies van der Rohe's prominent work in architecture and furniture characterized the International Style, an elegant variety of Classic Modernism.

Jasper Morrison
born 1959 London
96, 97

1979-1982: attended the Kingston School of Art; 1982-1985: graduated from the Royal College of Art, London; 1984: received a scholarship to the Berlin Academy of Arts; 1986: opened his own design studio; 1987: designed the installation for Reuter's News Center at "documenta 8," Kassel; 1988: installation "Some New Items for the House I" in Berlin; 1989: installation "Some New Items for the House II" for Vitra GmbH in Milan; 1992: published "A World Without Words"; received the german Bundespreis für Produktdesign award for a series of door handles created for Franz Schneider Brakel GmbH; 1993: installation for the Museum of Applied Art, Vienna; 1995: solo exhibition in the architectural center Arc en rêve, Bordeaux; numerous teaching positions and workshops.
Jasper Morrison's industrial and furniture designs have helped define the term "new simplicity."

George Nelson
born 1908 Hartford, Connecticut
died 1986 New York, New York
62, 63

1931: degree in architecture from Yale University; 1932-1934: studied at the American Academy, Rome; 1936-1941: together with William Hanby opened an architectural studio in New York; 1935-44: chief editor of the magazine Architectural Forum; 1945: published Tomorrow's House; 1946: established his own studio for architecture and industrial design; designed the "Basic Storage Components" shelf system; 1946-1966: director of design at Herman Miller Furniture Company, where he succeeded Gilbert Rohde; 1953: published "Chairs"; 1957: published Problems of Design; 1958: designed the Comprehensive Storage System for Herman Miller Furniture Company; 1964: designed several pavilions at the New York world's fair; 1968: designed the "Editor" typewriter for Olivetti; 1968-1975: member of the Conseil supérieur de la création industrielle, Paris; 1977: published "How to See"; 1983: designed the exhibition 'Design since 1945' at the Philadelphia Museum of Art.
In his theoretical and practical work, in particular as an architect and furniture designer, and in his numerous lectures, he incorporated fundamental social and cultural questions into his approach to design and gave them an international slant.

Verner Panton
born 1926 Gamtofte, Denmark
66, 69

1947-1951: studied architecture at the Royal Art Academy in Copenhagen; 1950-1952: worked in Arne Jacobsen's architectural studio; 1953-5: studied in various European countries; 1955: opened his own architecture and design studio; 1957: designed a cardboard house; 1963: moved to Switzerland; 1966: won the Rosenthal-Studio-Preis; 1968: exhibited his interior "Visiona" on the Bayer ship at the Cologne furniture fair; 1969: interior for the Spiegel publishing

company, Hamburg; participated in the exhibition "Qu'est-ce que le design" at Centre Georges Pompidou; 1974: interior for the Gruner & Jahr publishing company, Hamburg; 1984: visiting professor at the Offenbach College of Design; 1987 and 1988: retrospectives at the furniture fairs in Brussels and Copenhagen; 1994: several chair designs for the German company Polythema.
Verner Panton played a large part in defining the predominant color schemes used in the sixties and seventies. He has worked as a designer in the areas of furniture, lamps, fabrics, interiors, and exhibitions.

Charlotte Perriand
born 1903 Paris
27, 28, 29

Prior to 1925: studied interior design at École des Arts Décoratifs, Paris; 1926: presented metal furniture at the exhibition "Société des Artistes Décorateurs"; 1927-1937: worked with Le Corbusier and Pierre Jeanneret; 1929: presented her "L'équipement d'une habitation" at the Paris autumn salon; left Société des Artistes Décorateurs; joined Union des Artistes Modernes (UAM); 1930: together with Le Corbusier and Pierre Jeanneret participated in the first UAM exhibition; 1930 and 1933: traveled to the Soviet Union; 1940: together with Jean Prouvé set up an office for coordinating aspects of construction; 1940-1942: lived in Japan; until 1946: lived in Indochina; 1950: cofounder of the Formes Utiles group; active as an interior designer; 1958: with Jean Prouvé presented "La maison du Sahara" at Salon des Arts Ménagers; 1962-1968: traveled to South America; 1969: furnished the residence of the Japanese ambassador in Paris; 1993: presented a teahouse as part of the UNESCO event "Dialogue of the Cultures" in Paris.
Charlotte Perriand worked in Europe, Japan, and Brazil as an interior and furniture designer.

Gaetano Pesce
born 1939 La Spezia, Italy
77, 92

1959-1965: studied architecture and industrial design at the University of Venice; 1959: established Gruppo N in Padua; worked with similar groups of artists in Milan, Paris, and Germany; 1961: opened a studio with designer Milena Vettore; research in the area of serial and kinetic art; starting in 1962: active as an interior designer; 1969: designed a self-inflating furniture series for Cassina & Busnelli, Italy; 1971: established the company Bracciodiferro in order to manufacture experimental objects; 1972: participated in the exhibition "Italy: the New Domestic Landscape" at the MoMA, New York; starting in 1975: professor at the Institute for Architecture and Urban Planning in Strasbourg; 1978: project for a skyscraper in Manhattan; 1983: moved to New York; 1985-1987: professor at the Cooper Union School of Architecture and Art; 1987: Pluralist Tower project in Sao Paulo; 1989: designed mineral water bottles for Vittel, France; 1993: designed the offices of the Chiat Day advertising agency in New York; until 1995: extensive activity as an architect as well as a designer of interiors, furniture, and products; numerous additional teaching activities.
Gaetano Pesce has been a leading proponent of experimental design since the seventies.

Giancarlo Piretti
born 1940 Bologna, Italy
76

Degree in art education from the Bologna Art Academy; subsequently taught interior design at the same institution for seven years while simultaneously working as a furniture designer for Castelli; 1971: received the SMAU prize for the Plia chair; 1973: Gute Form award by the German Design Council, Darmstadt; 1975: advisory member of the ISIA Design College, Florence; 1980: National Industrial Design Award, United States; 1984-1986: worked for Castilia, a sub-

sidiary of Castelli; 1988: presented the "Piretti Collection," a seating system manufactured in the United States, Italy, Japan, Korea, Israel, Singapore, Venezuela, and Argentina; 1991: received the Compasso d'oro; 1994: Roscoe Award (U.S.) and G Mark (Japan) for the "Xylon" chair series.
Giancarlo Piretti works as furniture and industrial designer.

Gio (Giovanni) Ponti
born 1891 Milan
died 1979 Milan
55

Prior to 1921: studied architecture at the Milan Polytechnic; worked in the architectural studio of Mino Fiocchi and Emilio Lancia; 1923-1930: designs for the ceramic manufacturer Ricardo Ginori, in Doccia and Sesto Fiorentino; 1925-1979: directed the Monza Biennial; 1927: opened his own architectural studio in Milan together with Emilio Lancia; 1928: launched the magazine Domus, of which he was publisher until 1979; 1933: established the studio Ponti-Fornaroli-Soncini; received an Art Prize from the Italian Academy; 1936-1961: taught at Milan Polytechnic; 1941: initiated the magazine Stile; 1954: solo exhibition at the Institute of Contemporary Art, Boston; 1956: built the Pirelli Tower in Milan; Compasso d'oro; 1958: designed an administration building in Bagdad, Iraq; 1964: built the San Francesco church, Milan; 1968: honorary doctorate from the Royal College of Art, London; gold medal from the French Academy for Architecture; 1969: solo exhibition in the UCLA gallery, Los Angeles; 1970: built the Montedoria building in Milan; until 1976: comprehensive architectural activities; gave lectures on architecture worldwide.
As an architect, furniture designer, industrial designer, publisher, and professor, Gio Ponti was one of those men and women whose work led to the international fame of Italian design in the postwar era.

Jean Prouvé
born 1901 Paris, France
died 1984 Nancy, France
51

1916-21: apprenticed to two metal craftsmen in Paris, and studied at the École Supérieure, Nancy; 1923: opened his own smithy in Nancy; 1923-6: first furniture made of thin sheet steel; 1929: cofounder of Union des Artistes Modernes (UAM); 1930-1931: established the stock corporation Société des Ateliers Jean Prouvé; 1944: became mayor of Nancy following the end of German occupation; starting in 1947: opened Les Ateliers Jean Prouvé, a metal and aluminum processing plant in Maxéville (near Nancy) which manufactured steel girder constructions; 1957: the plant is acquired by Compagnie Industrielle de Matériel de Transport; professor at the CNAM in Paris; freelance architect in Paris; 1971: headed the jury for the design of the Centre Georges Pompidou, Paris.
Jean Prouvé emphasized visible metal constructions both in architecture and furniture design, and was thus an important forerunner of high-tech.

Heinz Rasch
born 1902
died 1996 Wuppertal
24

1916: attended the Arts and Crafts College Bromberg; 1920-1923: studied architecture in Stuttgart and Hanover; 1924: press spokesman for "Bauausstellung" in Stuttgart; 1925: editor of the magazine "Die Baugilde"; 1926-1930: worked as a freelance architect in Stuttgart; 1930: moved to Berlin; 1933: moved to Wuppertal; 1935-1945: advertising manager for the paint factory Kurt Herberts & Co. in Wuppertal; worked together with Willi Baumeister, Oskar Schlemmer and Franz Krause; 1956: proposed classifying the Weißenhof settlement as an historical monument.

Bodo Rasch
born 1903
died 1995 Leinfelden-Echterdingen
24

1922-1926: studied agriculture in Stuttgart-Hohenheim; 1923-1926: completed apprenticeship and worked as a joiner during his studies; 1930: freelance architect in Stuttgart; 1931: became member of CIAM; 1932-1933: published the "Stuttgarter Wochenspiegel" with his own contributions on architecture; 1933-1934: published the cultural magazine "Zirkel"; 1977: initiator and founding member of the association of the friends of the Weißenhof settlement.

Gerrit Thomas Rietveld
born 1888 Utrecht
died 1964 Utrecht
18, 20, 25, 38, 39

1899: trained as a carpenter in his father's workshop in Utrecht; 1904-1911: draftsman at a goldsmith's shop; attended evening classes at the Utrecht Museum of Arts and Crafts; 1906: pupil of the architect P. J. C. Klaarhamer; 1917: worked as a freelance cabinetmaker in Utrecht; 1918: became acquainted with Theo van Doesburg; joined the De Stijl group; 1919: opened his own architectural studio in Utrecht; first exhibitions with De Stijl; 1924: built the Schröder residence in Utrecht; 1927: began experimenting with new materials such as tubular steel, particle board, sheet aluminum, and laminated wood; 1928: cofounder of Congrès Internationaux d'Architecture Moderne (CIAM); 1947-1951: taught at the College of Art and Science, Rotterdam; 1950-1954: taught at the Art Academy of the Hague; 1951: major De Stijl retrospective in Amsterdam; numerous commissions; 1954: designed the Dutch pavilion at the Venice Biennial; 1954-1958: designed the building for the Institute of Applied Art, Amsterdam; 1958-1963: built the Arnheim Academy of Visual Arts; 1961: opened an architectural studio together with J. van Dillen and J. van Tricht; 1964: received an honorary doctorate from the Delft Polytechnic.

Furniture designer and architect Gerrit Rietveld was a major figure in rational Modernism and opened new doors in furniture construction through his experiments.

Jens Risom
born 1919, Denmark
47

1938: emigrated to the United States, textile drafts for Dan Cooper; first furniture drafts; 1939-1940: began working together closely with Hans Knoll; exhibition of interios furnishings together with the firm of Hans Knoll at the world fair in New York, one set for General Motors; 1941: trip throught the United States, together with Hans Knoll; several commissions on interior furnishings; 1942: publication of first Knoll catalogue, including furniture mainly by Jens Risom; 1943: joined the American forces; 1946: founding of design office Jens Risom Inc.; around 1955: worked together with Richard Avedon for advertising purposes on his own furniture designs; as of 1960: mainly designs for office furniture; 1970: acquisition of Jens Risom Inc. by the firm Dictaphone; 1979-1973: manager of Jens Risom Design Inc for Dictaphone; from 1973: founding of his own bureau Design Control in New Canaan, Connecticut.

David Rowland
born 1924 Los Angeles
70

1940-1943: studied under L. Moholy-Nagy at the Institute of Design in Chicago; 1943-1945: acted as pilot in the World War II; 1946-1949: studied at the Principia College of Liberal Arts, Elsah, Illinois; graduated in physics; 1950-1951: studied at the Cranbrook Academy of Art, Bloomfield Hills, Michigan; graduated as an industrial designer; 1951: first prize of the Illuminating Engineers Society; 1952-1953: worked in the bureau of designer Norman Bel Geddes; 1954: founded his own design bureau; interior décor for private rooms and business premises, chair drafts; 1957: first presentation of a draft at the Milan Triennial; 1964: Grand Prix from the Milan Triennial for the 40/4 chair; 1965: distinction from the American Institute of Designers (AID) and the Product Engineering Magazine; 1971: patenting of the material Soflex; 1979: gold medal from the Institute of Business Designers.

Eero Saarinen
born 1910 Kirkkonummi, Finland
died 1961 Ann Arbor, Michigan
46, 65

1923: the Saarinen family emigrated to the United States; 1929-1930: Eero Saarinen studied sculpture at the Académie de la Grande Chaumière, Paris; 1930-1934: studied architecture at Yale University, New Haven, Connecticut; 1934-1936: traveled throughout Europe; 1936: worked in his father's architectural studio and assisted him in his activities as a professor at the Cranbrook Academy of Art; 1940: began working with Charles Eames; together they won first prize for their Organic Armchair in the MoMA competition "Organic Design in Home Furnishings"; 1941: designs for Knoll International; 1948: won the Jefferson Memorial Competition; 1950: opened his own architectural studio; 1953-1955: built the chapel and auditorium for the Massachusetts Institute of Technology, Cambridge; 1957: built the Milwaukee War Memorial, Wisconsin; 1960: member of the American Academy of Arts and Letters; 1962: designed the TWA terminal at the John F. Kennedy Airport, New York.
In addition to his decisive impact on the world of architecture, Eero Saarinen also had a significant influence on American furniture design, not least of all through his close working relationship with Charles Eames.

Ettore Sottsass
born 1917 Innsbruck, Austria
89

1935-1939: studied architecture at Turin Polytechnic; until 1945: prisoner-of-war in Sarajevo; until 1949: involved with painting and sculpture; 1949-1952: worked on different projects in Sardinia and Turin; 1950-1955: Fourteen architectural projects to rebuild demolished cities in northern Italy for an insurance company; 1956: worked with George Nelson in New York; 1958-1992: chief consultant for product design at Olivetti; cooperation on the design for the first electronic computer, the Elea 9003; 1959: Compasso d'Oro for Elea 9003; 1960: opened his own office in Milan; 1961: extended trip to Asia; 1964-1965: designed the Valentine typewriter for Olivetti; 1966-1967: furniture designs for Poltronova; first use of laminated materials; also manufactured ceramics; 1969: Delta di oro prize for the "Valentine" typewriter; 1970: gave a series of lectures in Great Britain and Japan; honorary doctorate from the College of Art, London; 1972: designs for Alessi; participated in the exhibition "Italy: the New Domestic Landscape" at the MoMA, New York; 1973: cofounder of the Global Tools group; 1976: established Studio Alchimia; large retrospective of Sottsass' works in Berlin, Paris, Jerusalem, and Sydney; 1980: established Sottsass Associati; 1981: set up the Memphis group; 1985: quit Memphis; as of 1986: Sottsass Associati handles industrial design, interior design, and visual communication projects as well as numerous architectural projects worldwide.

For decades, Ettore Sottsass has been one of the most influential personalities on the international design front. In his extensive oeuvre, he has reinterpreted shapes and colors as expressive elements in architecture and design.

Philippe Starck
born 1949, Paris
99, 100

1966-8: studied at the École Centrale des Arts Décoratifs, Paris; 1968: established the Quasar company to produce inflatable objects; 1971-1972: artistic director at Pierre Cardin studio; 1979: furnished the Paris nightclub Les Bains-Douches; 1979: opened his own design studio in Monfort l'Amaury; 1980: launched his own production company, Starck Products; 1982: designed the private chambers of the president of France in the Elysée Palace; 1984: designed Café Costes in Paris; 1986: taught at the Domus Academy in Milan and at the École des Arts Décoratifs; 1988: Grand Prix National de la Création Industrielle; 1989: first architectural project implemented: administration buildings for the Asahi Brewery in Tokyo; designed the multifunctional building Nani Nani in Tokyo; 1990: designed the Teatriz restaurant in Paris and Green Baron office building in Tokyo; planned the Red Baron; 1992: Honor Award from the American Institute of Architects for the Paramount Hotel, New York; 1993: designed the prefabricated house Starckinette for the company Les 3 Suisses.
Philippe Starck works in nearly all areas of design and has also been active for a number of years as an architect. His enormous productivity and novel ideas have made him a star in the design world.

Mart Stam
born 1899 Purmerond, Holland
died 1986 Goldbach, Switzerland
22

Trained at the Rijksnormaalschool voor Tekenonderwijs in Amsterdam; periods of practical training with various architects; 1922: moved to Berlin; worked with Max Taut and Hans Poelzig; 1923: participated in a Bauhaus exhibition; 1925: returned to Amsterdam via Paris; 1926: drafted the first tubular steel chair without back legs; realization of a building for the Weißenhof settlement in Stuttgart; 1927: founding member of the Congrès Internationaux d'Architecture Moderne (CIAM) together with Gerrit Rietveld and Hendrik Berlage; 1928: participated in the exhibition "Der Stuhl" in Stuttgart; 1931-1932: worked as a town planner in Russia; 1934: returned to the Netherlands; in the period following worked as a freelance architect together with his wife Lotte Beese. Managed the Institute of Applied Art in Amsterdam, published the magazine Open Oog, co-founder of the Institute Goed Wonen; 1948-1953: principal of the State Universities of Applied Art in Dresden and Weißensee; subsequently returned to the Netherlands; 1966: gave up all public posts, moved to Switzerland. Mart Stam embodied a line of thought in modern architecture in which economy, public spirit and functionality are more important than aesthetic questions.

Stiletto (Frank Schreiner)
born 1959 Rüsselsheim, Germany
91

1979-80: worked as a locksmith for trucks and tanks; 1980-1981: studied mechanical engineering in Berlin; 1981: active as a "design practitiones," involved in experimental graphics and art; 1982-1986: studied visual communication in Berlin; 1987-1988: studied sculpture in Dusseldorf, where he a was master-class student at the College of Art; starting in 1987: exhibitions in Vienna, Zurich, Cologne, Stuttgart, New York; 1991: opened the Studio für Gestaltungsschäden; organized Prodomo in Vienna; 1992: case study in collaboration with the Association of System Consultants for Product Design: "Making the Existant visible" based on the example of the Zschoppau motorcycle plant. Stiletto represents an artistically subversive current within the German design scene.

Gruppo Strum
(Giorgio Ceretti, Piero Derossi, Ricardo Rosso)
74

1963: Gruppo Strum established; 1972: participated in the MoMA exhibition "Italy: the New Domestic Landscape," where it displayed the Pratone and Tornerai seating.

Studio 65
80

1965: Founding of Studio 65 as a group of young artists and students of architecture; founding members: Franco Audrito, Enzo Bertone, Paolo Morello, Paolo Rondelli, Roberta Garosci; 1966: new members: Ferruccio Tartaglia, Federico Prandi, Giovanni Isoardi, Giandomenico Raineiro; 1967: actively participated in the student movement; 1969: transferred to professional work in the fields of design, architecture, urban development; participating members: Franco Audrito; Athena Sampaniotou, Giancarlo Paci, Ferruccio Tartaglia, Adriana Ferroni, Anna Pozzo, Maria Schiappa, Yanis Skoulas, Adriano Vanara, Franco Cucchiarati, Roberto Gibello, Paolo Perotti, Angelica Sampaniotits, Anna Maria Rachetta, Gianni Arnaudo, Pier Vogliazzo, Elisa Vaccarino, Giorgio Vaccarino, Rosanna Pardini, Enrico Bettini, Danilo Riva; 1975: formed the group A.D. 65 with Franco Fusari, Giorgio Maffei and Ettore Ghinassi; 1976: founded a branch in the Middle East.
Studio 65 played an important role in Italy's radical design movement and is active in the fields of urban development, architecture and design.

Gerald Summers
born 1899 Alexandria, Egypt
died 1967
37

Trained in an engineering firm; subsequently worked at Marconi

Wireless Telegraph Company, Ltd.; furniture designs for his own residence at the end of the twenties; 1931: established the company Makers of Simple Furniture; 1933: worked exclusively as a furniture designer; collaborated with Jack Pritchard of the Isokon furniture company; exhibited his furniture designs in Bristol and London; 1940: the company was closed due to the shortage of wood during World War II; after 1945: established Gerald Summers Ltd., which sold ball bearings.

H. V. Thaden
49

The only available information is that a furniture manufacturer named Thaden Jordan Furniture Corporation existed in the United States during the forties, and that one of the proprietors was an H. V. Thaden.

Giuseppe Terragni
born 1904 Meda/Milan
died 1943 Como, Italy
40

1921-1926: studied architecture at the polytechnic college in Milan, founded the group Sette toegether with Figini, Frette, Larco, Libera, Pollini, Rava; 1928: realization of first draft: an apartment house in Como; joined the group MIAR (Movimento italiano architetti razionalisti); 1930: participated in the IV. Triennial Monza; 1933: participated in the IV. CIAM Congress in Athens; 1933-1935: built five residential buildings in Milan; 1936; built the Casa del Fascio in Como; further building activities; 1939: called up into the army. Giuseppe Terragni's works are regarded as the most significant results of rationalistic architecture in Italy.

Michael Thonet
born 1796 Boppard, Germany
died 1871 Vienna, Austria
2, 4

Trained as a carpenter and cabinetmaker in Boppard; 1819: opened his own furniture workshop; 1830: first experiments with laminated wood; 1842: his workshop in Boppard was impounded; moved to Vienna; granted a five-year royal patent to produce bent laminated wood; employed in the workshop of the Viennese furniture producer List; 1843: created chairs for the Liechtenstein Palace; 1849: opened his own workshop in Vienna; 1850: designed chairs for the Daum café in Vienna; 1851: received a bronze medal at the London world's fair for his furniture designs; 1852: opened a sales office in Vienna; 1852: received a second patent for bending laminated wood; 1853: transferred ownership of the company to his sons under the name Gebrüder Thonet; 1855: participated in the Paris world's fair; first orders from overseas; 1856: established the first furniture plant in Korichan, Moravia; Austrian citizenship; granted the "patent for the solid bending of chairs and table legs"; 1858: closed down the Viennese workshop; opened a second sales office in Vienna; began producing chair No. 14; 1862: established a second factory in Bistritz, Czechoslovakia; 1866: set up a third plant in Gross-Ugrocs, Hungary.
In his role as an inventor and entrepreneur, Michael Thonet was one of the founding fathers of modern furniture production.

Henry van de Velde
born 1863 Antwerpen
died 1957 Zurich
7

1881-1884: studied painting at the Academy of Fine Arts in Antwerpen; 1884-1885: studied painting under Carolus Duran in Paris; 1889: joined the artists' group "Les XX"; first contact to the

ideas of the Arts & Crafts movement; typographic design of the magazine Van Nu en Straks; 1892/93: first publications and lectures on topics of art and craft; 1895: constructed his own house Bloemenwerf; interior furnishings for the art studio Salon de l'Art Nouveau belonging to the Parisian art dealer Samuel Bing; 1896: founded the Société van de Velde in order to produce his own drafts; 1897: presented furniture drafts at the art and crafts exhibition Dresden; 1899: presented over 60 drafts at the secession exhibition Munich; 1900: moved to Berlin; fitted out the Habana tobacco company, Berlin; 1901: appointed artistic adviser for industry, arts and crafts to the grand duchy of Saxony-Weimar; 1904: teaching assignment at the arts and crafts college Weimar; 1907: member of the German works association; 1908: re-establishing of the arts and crafts college Weimar; 1914: built theatre premises for the works association exhibition in Cologne; 1917: moved to Switzerland; 1921: moved to Holland; planned museum premises for the private collector Kröller-Müller; 1924: returned to Belgium; 1926: founded and managed the Institut Supérieur des Arts Décoratifs in Brussels; 1926-1932: teaching assignment in architecture at Gent University; 1947: moved to Switzerland.
Henry van de Velde was one of the most important representatives of Art Nouveau and even well into the Twenties exercised great influence on arts, crafts and design in Europe.

Robert Venturi
born 1925 Philadelphia, Pennsylvania
88

Degree in architecture from Princeton University; 1954-1956: studied at the American Academy, Rome; worked with Eero Saarinen; 1963: built the Chestnut Hill house in Philadelphia, Pennsylvania; 1964: together with John Rauch opened an architectural studio in Philadelphia; 1964: professor of architecture at Yale University; 1965: designed the Guild House in Philadelphia, Pennsylvania; 1966: published Complexity and Contradiction in Architecture; 1972: published Learning from Las Vegas; 1976: built the Allen Memorial

Art Museum, Oberlin, Ohio; 1985: published A View from the Campidoglio; awarded Firm of the Year prize by the American Institute of Architects; 1990: built the Institute for Economics at Princeton University; until 1991: built the annex to the National Gallery, London.
Architect and theorist Robert Venturi is a leading proponent of Postmodernist architecture.

Otto Wagner
born 1841 Penzing, Austria
died 1918 Vienna
15

1857-1862: studied architecture at the Polytechnic Institute in Vienna and at the Royal Building Academy Berlin, subsequently at the Academy of Fine Arts Vienna; 1862: joined the bureau of Heinrich von Förster; as of 1863: realization of numerous drafts; 1881: participated in a collective exhibition in the art house of Vienna; 1890: published the first volume of "Some sketches, projects and proven constructions" about his own creations; 1893: drafted a general regulation plan for the city of Vienna; 1894: appointed head of the planning department and building control office and head of the arts planning department of the Commission on Viennese traffic systems and the Danube Regulation Commission; appointed professor and head of a specialized school for architecture at the Academy of Fine Arts Vienna; 1895: published lectures from the first year under the title "Modern Architecture"; appointed member of the standing arts commission and of the arts council in the Department of Culture and Education; 1897: representative of the Academy at the international architectural congress in Brussels; became acquainted with van de Velde and the works of Paul Hankar and Tervueren; 1898: participated in the Viennese jubilee exhibition; 1899: split up from the art house association; membership of the Viennese secession; 1900: member of the jury at the world exhibition in Paris; 1903: participated in the founding of the association of Austrian architects; 1904-1906: new building of the Austrian Post Office

savings bank; 1908: president of the international architectural congress in Vienna; 1912: awarding of the title of Hofrat (Counsellor); 1917: first monograph on Otto Wagner by J.A. Lux.
As an architect and teacher Otto Wagner was a leading figure in the transition from the architecture of the 19 century to the modern age.

Hans J. Wegner
born 1914 Tonder, Denmark
72

Trained as a cabinetmaker; subsequently studied at Copenhagen Technical College; 1936-1938: studied furniture designs at Copenhagen Vocational Art's College; 1938-1940: worked in the architectural studio of Erik Moller and Flemming Lassen; 1943: employed in the architectural studio of Arne Jacobsen and Erik Moller in Arhus, where he designed furniture for the Arhus City Hall; first collaboration with cabinetmaker Johannes Hansen; 1943-1946: opened his own studio in Arhus; 1946-1948: worked for architect Palle Suenson in Copenhagen, then returned to his own office; 1946-1953: taught at Copenhagen Vocational Art's College; 1948: participated in the MoMA competition for "Low-Cost Furniture Design"; 1950: international breakthrough with the publication of Runde Stol in the American magazine Interior; large commission in the United States; 1951: Lunning Prize; 1954: Milan Triennial Gold Medal; starting in the mid-fifties: industrial production of Wegner's designs by Fritz Hansen and Salesco.
Hans J. Wegner helped bridge the gap between craftsmanship and industrial production, and contributed with his first-class furniture to the international reputation of Danish design.

Stefan Wewerka
born 1928 Magdeburg, Germany
86

Studied architecture, since 1947: has worked in the fields of architecture and housing scheme construction; 1954: ground archi-

tecture; as of 1961: worked as a sculptor and painter; numerous artistic-alienating chair installations; 1970: worked as a film director; 1974: first reproduction of a chair from an installation of Wewerka by the firm Tecta; since 1977: has worked with the firm Tecta; as of 1979: fashion drafts; 1981: jewelry drafts for Cleto Munari; 1987: drafted an attendant's seat for the "documenta 8".
Wewerka's unconventional furniture drafts are grouped between art and functional design and they characterised a young generation of German designers in the Eighties.

Frank Lloyd Wright
born 1867 Richland, Wisconsin
died 1959 Phoenix, Arizona
16, 19

1885-1887: studied engineering at the Engineering School of Wisconsin; 1888-1893: worked as a draftsman for architect Louis Sullivan in Chicago; 1893: opened his own architectural studio; 1897: cofounder of the Chicago Art and Crafts Society; 1900-1901: lectured; 1901: designed the Prairie House 1904: built administration buildings out of reinforced concrete for Larkin Company in Buffalo, New York; 1905: first trip to Japan; 1909: traveled to Europe, where he gave a great number of lectures; 1910-1911: German-language publication entitled "Buildings and Designs of Frank Lloyd Wright" published by Ernst Wasmuth; 1911: established the Spring Green community and built his own residence in Taliesin; 1912: built his first skyscraper; 1918: published the lecture "The Art and Craft of the Machine" in the magazine De Stijl; 1915-1922: designed and furnished the Imperial Hotel, Tokyo; 1929: built St. Mark's Tower in New York; honorary member of the Berlin Art Academy; 1936: designed the Fallingwater house in Bear Run, Pennsylvania; 1939: received a Royal Institute of British Architects gold medal; 1940: published An Organic Architecture; 1943: designed the Guggenheim Museum, New York; 1955: designed a furniture collection for mass production; 1959: built the Guggenheim Museum, New York.
The oeuvre of architect and designer Frank Lloyd Wright is one of the

most important and varied in the twentieth century. His visionary ideas influenced a great many architects of subsequent generations.

Sori Yanagi
born 1915 Tokyo
58

Prior to 1940: studied painting and architecture at the State University for Art and Music, Tokyo; 1940-1942: assistant to Charlotte Perriand in Japan; 1947: studied industrial design; 1951: first prize in the "First Japanese Industrial Design Competition" for a combination turntable/radio; 1952: founded the Yanagi Institute for Industrial Design in Tokyo; 1954: chair of industrial design at the Kanazawa Vocational Arts University; 1957: received a Milan Triennial Gold Medal; 1964: exhibited his works at "documenta 3," Kassel; 1977: director of the Japanese Museum of Folk Art in Tokyo.
Sori Yanagi worked predominantly as an industrial designer.

Marco Zanuso
born 1916 Milan
68

Prior to 1939: studied architecture in Milan; 1945: opened his own office in Milan; 1947-1949: chief editor of Casabella magazine; 1951: received Milan Triennial Gold Medal; 1958-1977: joint studio with Richard Sapper; active as an architect, industrial designer, and interior designer; 1966-1969: cofounder and president of the Associazione di Disegno Industriale (ADI); as of 1976: professor of industrial architecture at the Milan Polytechnic.
Marco Zanuso works as an architect, interior decorator, and industrial designer.

In the form of travelling exhibitions, workshops and publications, **Vitra Design Museum** undertakes to familiarize the public with the history of furniture and interior design as well as architecture.

Frank O. Gehry, one of the most renowned contemporary US architects, created the Museum in 1989. His first European building, it provides an inspired setting for the exhibitions. The Museum's standing collection houses over 2000 objects and comprises one of the most comprehensive documentation of industrial furniture design in the world. The focal points are bentwood furniture, designs by Viennese architects, the Bauhaus, De Stijl, US and Scandinavian design, plastic furniture, design by the

Memphis group, and contemporary design trends. The collection is backed up by an archive containing original drawings, journals, sales catalogs and photographs.

The Vitra Design Museum is an independent foundation and is mainly self-supporting, using the funds generated by its own activities.

On the Vitra Company grounds, next to Gehry's Museum building is Zara Hadid's fire station, a pavilion by Tadao Ando, and production facilities by Nicolas Grimshaw and Alvaro Siza. Visitors can participate in guided architectural tours and tours of the Museum in several different languages.

Vitra Design Museum - Shop

Miniatures Collection

A selection of Vitra Design Museum's extensive collection is now available for collectors and people interested in design in the form of miniatures. The collection is constantly being expanded and includes all the key items of international design history from 1850 to the present. Each miniature is true to the original in terms of construction, materials, and colors. Long development work is necessary to adapt the technology to meet the needs of miniature production. The miniatures are not only collector's items for furniture lovers, but also constitute ideal visual materials for use in universities and design academies.

At present, 35 models at scale 1 to 6 are available.

100 Masterpieces from the Vitra Design Museum Collection

An overview of over 150 years of furniture design that includes portraits of the designers and a seperate bibliography for each object. The 100 exhibition pieces are grouped according to central themes: Technology, Construction, Reduction, Organic Design, Decoration and Manifesto. Reproductions of original documents and detailed texts provide explanations of the history and context of each object.

272 pages with 450 illustrations, 23 x 30 cm
Available in German, English, French, Japanese, and Spanish.

CD-ROM "100 Masterpieces"

A virtual tour of the Vitra Design Museum and the "100 Masterpieces" exhibition, programmed with Quick Time-VR. For every object, the user can call up historical documents, detailed texts or short videos. Rotating models of the individual chairs convey the uniqueness of the objects.

In German and English, for Windows or Apple Macintosh

Poster "Vitra Design Museum Collection"

A representative selection of objects from the collection of the Vitra Design Museum documents the international history of modern furniture design from 1830 to the present day.
Format: 119 x 84 cm, 224 colour reproductions

Products and Information

Vitra Design Museum
Charles-Eames-Str. 1
D-79576 Weil am Rhein
Phone + 49 (0) 7621-7023578
Fax + 49 (0) 7621-7023146
http:// www. design-museum.de

Photos
Richard Bryant, Maxim Meekes, Thomas Dix, Grund + Flum